SECOND GEOLOGICAL SURVEY OF PENNSYLVANIA:
1874--5.

REPORT OF PROGRESS

IN THE

LABORATORY OF THE SURVEY

AT

HARRISBURG,

By ANDREW S. M'CREATH

HARRISBURG:
PUBLISHED BY THE BOARD OF COMMISSIONERS
FOR THE SECOND GEOLOGICAL SURVEY.
1875.

Entered, for the Commonwealth of Pennsylvania, in the year 1875, according
to acts of Congress,
BY JOHN B. PEARSE,
Secretary of the Board of Commissioners of Geological Survey.
In the Office of the Librarian of Congress, at
WASHINGTON, D. C.

Stereotyped by
Singerly Printing and Publishing House,
Harrisburg, Pa.

Printed by
B. F. MEYERS, *State Printer*,
HARRISBURG, PA.

BOARD OF COMMISSIONERS.

His Excellency, JOHN F. HARTRANFT, *Governor*,
and *ex-officio* President of the Board, Harrisburg.

ARIO PARDEE,	Hazleton.
WILLIAM A. INGHAM,	Philadelphia.
HENRY S. ECKERT,	Reading.
HENRY M'CORMICK,	Harrisburg.
JAMES MACFARLANE,	Towanda.
JOHN B. PEARSE,	Philadelphia.
ROBERT B. WILSON, M. D.,	Clearfield.
Hon. DANIEL J. MORRELL,	Johnstown.
HENRY W. OLIVER,	Pittsburg.
SAMUEL Q. BROWN,	Pleasantville.

SECRETARY OF THE BOARD

JOHN B. PEARSE, - - - - - Philadelphia.

STATE GEOLOGIST

PETER LESLEY, - - - - - Philadelphia.

LABORATORY OF THE GEOLOGICAL SURVEY,
223 MARKET STREET,
HARRISBURG *October 1st*, 1875.

Prof. J. P. Lesley,
    State Geologist:

Sir:—I have the honor herewith to submit my report of the operations in the Laboratory of the Survey, at Harrisburg, during the past and present year; with a brief description of the methods of analysis employed.

The work of organizing the Laboratory was commenced in August, 1874; but much time was necessarily spent in fitting up and in procuring the proper chemicals and apparatus; so that actual analytical work was not begun until about the middle of September, 1874.

The number of analyses required for the reports of the assistant geologists has been too great to permit any considerable amount of original investigation.

Many tests, qualitative and otherwise, have been made, the results of which are not here-recorded; but it is believed that nothing of interest or importance has been omitted from these tables.

I would avail myself of this opportunity to express my thanks to Mr. S. A. Ford, who has assisted me in the Laboratory since May, 1875,—all the analyses made by him being given over his name; and also to Mr. Frederick W. Forman for much valuable assistance rendered.

        Yours, very respectfully,
            Andrew S. M'Creath.

TABLE OF CONTENTS

	PAGE.
CHAPTER I. Bituminous coals, cokes, &c.,	1
CHAPTER II. Iron ores,	43
Section 1. Method of analysis,	43
Section 2. Brown hematite ores of Lehigh county. Silurian,	48
Section 3. Iron ores of York county. Cambrian (?) and Mesozoic,	55
Section 4. Fossil ores of the Juniata. Silurian,	60
Section 5. Brown hematite ores of the Juniata. Devonian,	64
Section 6. Brown hematite ores of the Coal Measures,	68
Section 7. Carbonate ores of the Juniata. Devonian,	69
Section 8. Carbonate ores of the Coal Measures,	71
CHAPTER III. Limestones,	75
CHAPTER IV. Fire-clays,	78
CHAPTER V. Miscellaneous analyses	89

REPORT OF PROGRESS

IN

THE LABORATORY AT HARRISBURG.

1874-'75.

BY ANDREW S. M'CREATH, CHEMICAL ASSISTANT.

CHAPTER I.

BITUMINOUS COALS.

The term *bituminous* is usually applied to those coals which yield a large percentage of volatile combustible matter, and which burn with more or less of a yellow smoky flame. They are generally brittle, with a bright shining or resinous lustre, and a black or brownish-black color. Under the name bituminous, however, are included a number of kinds, which differ materially under the action of heat, giving rise to the general classification, *caking* or *coking coals*, and *free-burning coals*. *Coking coals* are those which, when heated strongly in a covered vessel, become partially fused and agglomerate into a mass of coherent coke. *Free-burning coals*, on the other hand, are those which, on being heated in a covered vessel, do not fuse or cake together in any sensible degree, and whose particles do not unite to form a coherent coke. The manner of treating the coal, however, influences in a marked degree its coking qualities, since some coals which, when treated in the usual way, are practically non-coking, when rapidly exposed in a closed vessel to a very high heat, yield a firm coherent coke.

The term *semi-bituminous* is applied to that class of coals which, while they yield combustible gases and a coke, never contain more than eighteen per cent volatile combustible matter. According to this classification, therefore, all the coals examined during the past season are strictly bituminous. As a class they are characterized by possessing a bright shining or resinous lustre, a tendency to columnar structure, and by yielding a coherent coke when strongly heated in a closed vessel.

The analyses given in the following tables are what are commonly known as "proximate" analyses. By a general or proximate analysis we determine the following ingredients:—Water, volatile combustible matter, fixed carbon, sulphur and ash.

The method of analysis used is the following:

Method of Analysis.

1. *Determination of Water.*—A weighed quantity of the coal was put into a counterpoised watch glass and dried in an air-bath, heated to a temperature of 225° to 230° F., until no further loss in weight occurred. An hour was generally sufficient for this purpose. The watch glass and contents were then rapidly transferred to a desiccator, where they were allowed to cool thoroughly. The weight was then taken, and the loss noted as water.

2. *Volatile matter.*—A weighed quantity of the coal, in coarse powder, was placed in a platina crucible, fitted loosely with a lid, and heated to a red heat over a Bunsen gas burner until the flame of the escaping gas was no longer visible; it was then exposed to a nearly white heat for five minutes. After being allowed to cool thoroughly in the desiccator, the crucible and contents were again weighed, and the loss in weight, after deducting the water found in the previous experiment, was put down as volatile matter.

3. *Ash.*—The coke remaining in the crucible was heated over a Bunsen burner, or in a muffle, until all the combustible matter was burned off. The color of the ash was then noted, and its weight determined in the usual way.

4. *Sulphur.*—One gramme of the coal, finely pulverized, was fused with ten grammes of carbonate of soda, and six grammes nitrate of potash, until fusion was calm. The mass was then dissolved in water, the solution acidulated with hydrochloric acid, and evaporated to dryness; re-dissolved in dilute hydrochloric acid, diluted with distilled water, filtered, and the sulphuric acid precipitated by means of chloride of barium. The solution was now allowed to stand over for twelve hours, when

the sulphate of baryta was filtered off, dried, ignited and weighed; from the weight of this the per cent of sulphur was readily calculated.

5. *Fixed Carbon.*—This was estimated by deducting the percentage of water, volatile matter, ash and sulphur found, from 100, and taking the "difference" as fixed carbon.

Notes.—It may be here stated that it was found impossible to obtain carbonate of soda perfectly free from sulphur, so that a separate test had to be made of that re-agent, and the proper deductions allowed.

As many of the samples of coal had been taken several months previous to analysis, it has been thought desirable to affix to each specimen the date of sampling and analysis, so that some estimate can be made as to the amount of drying each specimen had undergone previous to analysis. In this way some seeming discrepencies may be accounted for. For the sake of convenient reference, the letter and page of the report in which the geology of the specimen is given, are also added with each analysis.

Clearfield County.

	I.	II.	III.	IV.
Water	0.810	1.942	0.780	0.710
Volatile matter	20.640	22.720	21.680	23.400
Fixed carbon	74.023	71.018	73.052	72.218
Sulphur	.507	.543	.688	.532
Ash	4.020	3.777	3.800	3.140
	100.000	100.000	100.000	100.000
Coke, per cent	78.550	75.340	77.540	75.890
Color of ash	White.	Cream.	Gray.	Gray, with red tinge.

I. *Penn Colliery*, Houtzdale, five and a half miles south-west of Osceola.

The coal is deep black, with shining lustre, somewhat columnar structure, easily broken, the fragments having a somewhat cubical shape.

Sampled July 15th. Analyzed Sept. 7th.
Published in report of progress, 1874, H, page 29.

II. *Franklin Colliery*, Houtzdale, five and a half miles south-west of Osceola. (See Report of Progress, 1874, H, page 30.)

The coal is of a deep black color, shining lustre, somewhat columnar structure, very friable, and containing considerable mineral charcoal, also numerous small scales of calcite, and a small amount of iron pyrites.

Analyzed fresh from mine.

III. *Eureka Mine*, Houtzdale, five and a half miles southwest of Osceola. (See Report of Progress, 1874, H, page 32.) The coal is shiny black, with small seams of charcoal. Sampled July 15th. Analyzed Sept. 8th.

IV. *Stirling Mine*, Houtzdale, five and a half miles southwest of Osceola. (See Report of Progress, 1874, H, page 35.) The coal is black, columnar, and contains scales of iron pyrites. Sampled July 15th. Analyzed Sept. 15th.

	V.	VI.	VII.	VIII.
Water	0.765	1.100	1.100	0.700
Volatile matter	20.090	23.070	22.450	23.565
Fixed carbon	74.779	71.199	72.300	68.890
Sulphur	.666	.611	.....	1.715
Ash	3.700	4.020	4.150	5.130
	100.000	100.000	100.000	100.000
Coke, per cent	79.145	75.830	76.450	75.735
Color of ash	Gray.	Red.		Gray.

V. *Moshannon Colliery*, (Bed B) on Beaver branch of Moshannon, three and a half miles south-west of Osceola. (See Report of Progress, 1874, H, page 36.)

The coal is black, shining, friable, and contains iron pyrites and charcoal.

Sampled July 16th. Analyzed September 16th.

VI. *New Moshannon Mine*, north side of Beaver branch of Moshannon river, three and a half miles south-west of Osceola. (See Report of Progress, 1874, H, page 37.)

The coal has rather a dirty appearance, is friable, and contains iron pyrites.

Sampled July 16th. Analyzed October 9th.

VII. *Moshannon Coal*, analyzed by Messrs. Booth & Garrett, and published by permission of Mr. David Knight, president Moshannon Coal Company.

VIII. *Mapleton Colliery*, on Shimmel's run, one and a half

miles north of Osceola. (See Report of Progress, 1874, H, page 43.)

The coal has a shining lustre, columnar structure, is easily broken, and contains small scales of iron pyrites.

Sampled July 18th.   Analyzed October 9th.

	IX.	X.	XI.	XII.
Water	0.570	0.740	1.630	0.620
Volatile matter	24.630	25.210	22.000	22.135
Fixed carbon	68.400	68.628	72.815	68.728
Sulphur	1.900	2.122	.425	.867
Ash	4.500	3.300	3.130	7.650
	100.000	100.000	100.000	100.000
Coke, per cent	74.800	74.050	76.370	77.245
Color of Ash	Gray, red tinge.	Red.	Gray, red tinge.	Gray.

IX. *Hale's Colliery*, one mile north of Osceola. Upper bench. (See Report of Progress, 1874, H, page 42.)

The coal is bright, shining, columnar structure, with small seams of iron pyrites.

Sampled July 24th.   Analyzed October 24th.

X. *Hale's Colliery.* Lower bench. (See Report of Progress, 1874, H, page 42.)

The coal is bright, shining, columnar, with small veins of iron pyrites.

Sampled July 24th.   Analyzed October 24th.

XI. *Webster Colliery*, Goss Run branch of Tyrone and Clearfield railroad, five miles south-west of Osceola. (See Report of Progress, 1874, H, page 33.)

The coal has a bright resinous lustre, is of somewhat columnar structure, and friable. It contains numerous veins of bright crystalline coal and mineral charcoal, and shows little iron pyrites.

Analyzed fresh from mine.

XII. *Logan Colliery*, on Shimmel's run, two miles north, north-west of Osceola. (See Report of Progress, 1874, H, page 44.)

The coal has a dull lustre, somewhat columnar structure, with thin veins of slate running through it.

Sampled July 18th.   Analyzed October 9th

	XIII.	XIV.	XV.	XVI.
Water	0.800	0.640	0.820	0.410
Volatile matter	23.260	24.360	23.900	22.810
Fixed carbon	72.350	64.082	69.007	66.690
Sulphur	.590	3.378	1.373	1.790
Ash	3.000	7.540	4.900	8.300
	100.000	100.000	100.000	100.000
Coke, per cent	75.940	75.000	75.280	76.780
Color of Ash	Red.	Gray, p'k tinge.	Gray, p'k tinge.	Gray, p'k tinge.

XIII. *Laurel Run Colliery*, on Shimmel's run, two miles north, north-west of Osceola. (See Report of Progress, 1874, H, page 45.)

The coal has a bright shining lustre, columnar structure, containing small scales of iron pyrites. It yields a somewhat porous, friable coke when the coal is coked in a platina crucible.

Sampled July 18th. Analyzed October 9th.

XIV. *Decatur Coal Company's Colliery*, one and a half miles north of Philipsburg, Centre county. Lower bench. (See Report of Progress, 1874, H, page 48.)

The coal has a bright shining lustre, columnar structure, and contains considerable pyrites.

Sampled July 20th. Analyzed October 17th.

XV. *Decatur Coal Company's Colliery*. Upper bench. (See Report of Progress, 1874, H, page 49.)

The coal has a bright shining lustre and columnar structure.

Sampled July 20th. Analyzed October 17th.

XVI. *Derby Colliery*, one and a half miles west of Philipsburg. (See Report of Progress, 1874, H, page 47.)

The coal is bright, columnar, friable, and contains small veins of charcoal.

Sampled July 23d. Analyzed October 21st.

	XVII.	XVIII.	XIX.	XX.
Water	0.550	0.560	0.420	0.620
Volatile matter	24.090	25.190	25.010	22.730
Fixed carbon	71.689	71.013	67.221	68.794
Sulphur	.571	.587	2.479	1.576
Ash	3.100	2.650	4.870	6.280
	100.000	100.000	100.000	100.000
Coke, per cent	75.360	74.250	74.570	76.650
Color of Ash	Gray.	Salmon.	Pink.	Gray.

XVII. *Morrisdale Mine*, three miles north, north-west of Philipsburg. Lower bench. (See Report of Progress, 1874, H, page 50.)

The coal is bright, shining, columnar, with little pyrites.

Sampled July 20th. Analyzed October 19th.

XVIII. *Morrisdale Mine.* Upper bench. (See Report of Progress, 1874, H, page 50.)

The coal is bright, shining, with considerable pyrites.

Sampled July 20th. Analyzed October 21st.

XIX. *Hubler's Mine*, four miles north-west of Kylertown. (See Report of Progress, 1874, H, page 52.)

The coal has a bright shining lustre, friable, and contains veins of iron pyrites. Shows peculiar chisel-faced (oblique) forms.

Sample not freshly mined.

XX. *Williamson's Mine*, on Williamson's run, one mile east of Philipsburg, Centre county. (See Report of Progress, 1874, H, page 56.)

The coal is shining, columnar, contains veins of charcoal and pyrites. Coal is very compact and heavy.

Sampled July 23d. Analyzed October 21st.

	XXI.	XXII.	XXIII.	XXIV.
Water	0.540	0.600	0.650	0.630
Volatile matter	22.560	22.600	23.000	24.630
Fixed carbon	71.551	68.709	71.799	70.396
Sulphur	1.079	2.691	.551	.654
Ash	4.270	5.400	4.000	3.690
	100.000	100.000	100.000	100.000
Coke, per cent	76.900	76.800	76.350	74.740
Color of Ash	Light Gray.	Gray, p'k tinge.	Red.	Red.

XXI. *Powelton Mine*, three miles south-east of Osceola. Upper bench. (See Report of Progress, 1874, H, page 40.)

The coal has a comparatively dull lustre, is hard, with slate and iron pyrites in veins.

Sampled July 22d. Analyzed October 22d.

XXII. *Powelton Mine.* Lower bench. (R. P., 1874, H, p. 40.)

The coal is bright, shining, columnar, with small veins of pyrites and charcoal.

Sampled July 22d. Analyzed October 23d.

XXIII. *G. W. Davis' Mine*, one and a half miles south-east of Janesville, Clearfield county. (R. P., 1874, H, p. 102.)

The coal has a dead lustre, is friable, contains charcoal and pyrites in veins; slightly iridescent.

Sampled July 31st. Analyzed October 26th.

XXIV. *Reitur's Mine*, near Karthaus P. O. Upper bed. (R. P., 1874, H, p. 81.)

The coal is bright, shining, very hard, with small scales of iron pyrites.

Sampled August 17th. Analyzed October 29th.

	XXV.	XXVI.	XXVII.	XXVIII.
Water	0.750	0.380	0.550	0.480
Volatile matter	19.570	22.280	22.650	22.320
Fixed carbon	69.833	67.995	72.616	59.788
Sulphur	.677	2.455	1.334	4.232
Ash	9.170	6.890	2.850	13.180
	100.000	100.000	100.000	100.000
Coke, per cent	79.680	77.340	76.800	77.200
Color of Ash		Gray, red tinge.	Dirty gray.	Red.	Pinkish.

XXV. *Mon's Mine*, one-half mile south of Kylertown. (R. P., 1874, H, p. 86.)

The coal is hard and compact, with dull resinous lustre.

Sampled August 18th. Analyzed October 30th.

XXVI. *Hill's Mine*, two-thirds mile east of Clearfield. (R. P., 1874, H, p. 90.)

The coal is shining, columnar, with much iron pyrites and charcoal in veins.

Sampled August 19th. Analyzed October 30th.

XXVII. *Mason's Mine*, one and a half miles west of Clearfield. Upper bench. (R. P., 1874, H, p. 91.)

The coal is bright, columnar, containing veins of charcoal and iron pyrites.

Sampled August 20th. Analyzed November 2d.

XXVIII. *Mason's Mine*. Lower bench. (R. P., 1874, H, p. 91.)

The coal has a glossy lustre, is very friable, and contains much pyrites.

Sampled August 20th. Analyzed November 2d.

ANALYSES OF BITUMINOUS COALS.

	XXIX.	XXX.	XXXI.	XXXII.
Water	0.410	0.520	0.870	0.700
Volatile matter	21.800	21.030	21.680	24.020
Fixed carbon	72.903	67.133	68.928	64.951
Sulphur	1.087	.767	1.302	1.639
Ash	3.800	10.550	7.220	8.690
	100.000	100.000	100.000	100.000
Coke, per cent	77.790	78.450	77.450	75.280
Color of Ash	Reddish.	Reddish gray.	Pinkish.	Red.

XXIX. *Humphrey's Mine*, one mile west of Clearfield. (R. P., 1874, H, p. 91.)

The coal is bright, friable, fracture showing chisel-faced (oblique) forms; pyrites in veins.

Sampled August 20th. Analyzed November 2d.

XXX. *J. Shaw's Mine*, one mile north, north-west of Clearfield. Lower bench. (R. P., 1874, H, p. 92.)

The coal is bright, shining, very hard, with slate and charcoal in veins.

Sampled August 20th. Analyzed November 4th.

XXXI. *R. Shaw's Mine*, one and one-fourth mile north of Clearfield. (R. P., 1874, H, p. 93.)

The coal has a dull lustre, columnar structure, is very friable, and contains pyrites and charcoal.

Sampled August 30th. Analyzed November 3d.

XXXII. *J. Cooper's Mine*, one mile south-east of Glen Hope, Clearfield creek. (R. P., 1874, H, p. 105.)

The coal has a dull lustre, very hard, and shows much oxide of iron and iron pyrites.

Sampled July 31st. Analyzed October 27th.

	XXXIII.	XXXIV.	XXXV.
Water	0.860	0.940	0.950
Volatile matter	31.600	31.060	32.450
Fixed carbon	61.662	61.563	59.904
Sulphur	2.288	1.487	1.296
Ash	3.590	4.950	5.400
	100.000	100.000	100.000
Coke, per cent	67.540	68.000	66.600
Color of Ash	Brown, red specks.	Gray, red tinge.	Gray.

XXXIII. *Mongold's Mine*, Bell township, four miles south-east of Troutville. (R. P., 1874, H, p. 115.)

The coal has a bright shining lustre, is rather compact, and shows little pyrites.

Sampled September 24th. Analyzed January 26th.

XXXIV. *Tyler's Mine*, Tyler's station, on Low Grade railroad, (Bennett's Branch.) (R. P., 1874, H, p. 140.)

The coal is bright, friable, containing slate, charcoal and pyrites.

Sampled November 19th. Analyzed November 27th.

XXXV. *Bell's Mine*, near Evergreen station, on the Low Grade railroad, seven miles north-east of Reynoldsville. (R. P., 1874, H, p. 192.)

The coal is bright, compact, and contains charcoal and pyrites.

Sampled September 11th. Analyzed November 14th.

Centre County.

	XXXVI.	XXXVII.	XXXVIII.
Water	1.280	0.650	0.750
Volatile matter	25.580	24.560	23.440
Fixed carbon	68.937	70.416	64.374
Sulphur	.613	.964	.986
Ash	3.590	3.410	10.450
	100.000	100.000	100.000
Coke, per cent	73.140	74.790	76.800
Color of Ash	Cream.	Cream.	Gray, red tinge.

XXXVI. *Snow Shoe Mines*, Mine No. 5, Upper bed. (R. P., 1874, H, p. 71.)

The coal is compact, with a shining lustre, very hard, and contains small veins of charcoal.

Sampled August 6th. Analyzed October 28th.

XXXVII. *Snow Shoe Mine*, No. 6, Middle bed. (R. P, 1874, H, p. 70.)

The coal has a resinous lustre, and contains thin veins of pyrites and charcoal.

Sampled August 6th. Analyzed October 28th.

XXXVIII. *Snow Shoe Basin*, Mine No. 4, (Lower bed,) B. (R. P., 1874, H, p. 70.)

The coal is bright, shining, and contains veins of charcoal and pyrites. Iridescent.

Sampled August 7th. Analyzed October 29th.

ANALYSES OF BITUMINOUS COALS.

	XXXIX.	XL.
Water	0.880	1.680
Volatile matter	23.620	21.870
Fixed carbon	70.089	71.108
Sulphur	.661	.612
Ash	4.750	4.730
	100.000	100.000
Coke, per cent	75.500	76.450
Color of Ash	Red.	Red.

XXXIX. *William Holt's Mine*, west of Holt's Hill, two miles north-west of Snow Shoe City. Bottom bench of bed; lower hard part of bench. (R. P., 1874, H, p. 74.)

The coal has a dull lustre generally, and shows considerable iridescence.

Sampled August 6th. Analyzed October 27th.

XL. *William Holt's Mine*, Snow Shoe basin, two miles north-west of Snow Shoe City. (R. P., 1874, H, p. 74.)

The coal has a shining lustre generally; some pieces dull lustre, iridescent.

Sampled August 6th. Analyzed October 27th.

Jefferson County.

	XLI.	XLII.	XLIII.	XLIV.
Water	1.120	0.980	0.950	1.190
Volatile matter	33.860	30.300	35.130	32.810
Fixed carbon	60.692	50.521	59.304	55.316
Sulphur	1.278	2.429	1.436	2.284
Ash	3.050	15.770	3.180	8.400
	100.000	100.000	100.000	100.000
Coke, per cent	65.020	68.720	63.920	66.000
Color of Ash	Gray, red tinge.	Gray, red tinge.	Dirty gray.	Gray, p'k tinge.

XLI. *Diamond Colliery*, (formerly D. Reynold's mine,) one mile north of Reynoldsville. Lower part of "six foot bench" worked. (R. P., 1874, H, p. 151.)

The coal has a dead lustre on outer surface, contains charcoal and pyrites.

Sampled August 28th. Analyzed November 7th.

XLII. *Diamond Colliery.* Upper part of six foot bench. (R. P., 1874, H, p. 152.)

The coal has a dull resinous lustre, contains charcoal and much iron pyrites.

Sampled August 28th.   Analyzed November 7th.

XLIII. *Diamond Colliery.* Main five foot bench. (R. P., 1874, H, p. 152.)

The coal has a dull resinous lustre generally, but with veins of bright crystalline coal running through the mass; is rather hard, and contains soft mineral charcoal.

Sampled August 28th.   Analyzed November 7th.

XLIV. *Diamond Colliery.* Middle bench; the 23 inch coal above the six foot bench.

The coal has a shining lustre, is compact and hard, and contains veins of iron pyrites.

	XLV.	XLVI.	XLVII.	XLVIII.
Water	1.100	1.100	1.100	0.960
Volatile matter	29.990	32.900	30.800	32.680
Fixed carbon	46.639	62.174	62.524	59.097
Sulphur	3.101	.726	.776	1.063
Ash	19.170	3.100	4.800	6.200
	100.000	100.000	100.000	100.000
Coke, per cent	68.910	66.000	68.100	66.360
Color of Ash	Gray, red tinge.	Cream.	Cream.	Gray, red tinge.

XLV. *Diamond Colliery*, one mile north of Reynoldsville. Upper bench (the 25 inch coal) not worked. (R.. P, 1874, H, p 153.)

The coal has a dull lustre, is hard and compact, with veins of pyrites and much slate.

Sampled August 28th.   Analyzed November 7th.

XLVI. *Hoover's Mine,* (Ohio Co.,) Reynoldsville. Lower part of six foot bench worked. (R. P., 1874, H, p. 155.)

The coal has a shining lustre, is compact, with thin veins of charcoal, pyrites and slate.

Sampled August 29th.   Analyzed November 9th.

XLVII. *Hoover's Mine.* Middle part of six foot bench worked. (R. P., 1874, H, p. 154.)

The coal has a dull resinous lustre, is very hard, and contains charcoal and iron pyrites.

Sampled August 29th.   Analyzed November 13th.

XLVIII. *Hoover's Mine.* Upper part of six foot bench worked. (R. P., 1874, H, p. 154.)

ANALYSES OF BITUMINOUS COALS.

The coal is hard and compact, has a dull lustre, and contains pyrites in thin layers.

Sampled August 29th.   Analyzed November 13th.

	XLIX.	L.	LI.	LII.
Water	1.440	1.600	1.480	1.430
Volatile matter	32.460	30.700	29.220	31.940
Fixed carbon	63.011	63.791	65.022	62.109
Sulphur	.639	.639	.608	.531
Ash	2.450	3.270	3.670	3.990
	100.000	100.000	100.000	100.000
Coke, per cent	66.100	67.700	69.300	66.630
Color of Ash	Cream.	Red.	Gray, red tinge.	Cream.

XLIX. *Woodward Reynolds' Mine*, one mile south of Reynoldsville. (R. P., 1874, H, p. 157.)

The coal has a shining lustre, is compact, with a small amount of iron pyrites.

Sampled September 22d.   Analyzed January 6th.

L. *Shiesley's Bank*, half a mile south of Reynoldsville. Upper part of worked bench. (R. P., 1874, H, p. 158.)

The coal has a resinous lustre, is compact and hard; slightly iridescent, and contains iron pyrites in veins.

Sampled August 28th.   Analyzed November 5th.

LI. *Shiesley's Bank.* Lower part worked coal. (R. P., 1874, H, p. 158.)

The coal has a resinous lustre, is very hard, and contains considerable iron pyrites.

Sampled August 28th.   Analyzed November 6th.

LII. *Sprague's Coal Mine*, three miles east of Reynoldsville. (R. P., 1874, H, p. 161.)

The coal is shining on outside, resinous on fresh fracture, with little iron pyrites.

Sampled October 2d.   Analyzed January 6th.

	LIII.	LIV.	LV.	LVI.
Water	0.850	1.040	0.960	1.300
Volatile matter	31.200	31.610	32.320	30.220
Fixed Carbon	59.882	62.464	58.640	63.617
Sulphur	1.368	.736	1.230	.763
Ash	6.700	4.150	6.850	4.100
	100.000	100.000	100.000	100.000
Coke, per cent	67.950	67.350	66.720	68.480
Color of Ash	Dirty Gray, red tinge.	Gray, red tinge.	Gray, pink tinge.	Lavender.

LIII. *Seley's Bank*, three and a half miles east of Reynoldsville. Upper four foot of worked coal. (R. P., 1874, H, p. 160.)

The coal has a dull rusty appearance, is hard, iridescent, and contains pyrites in veins.

Sampled August 27th. Analyzed November 4th.

LIV. *Seley's Bank.* Lower part of five foot bench worked. (R. P., 1874, H, p. 160.)

The coal has a dead lustre, is hard, iridescent, and contains small scales of sulphate of lime.

Sampled August 27th. Analyzed November 4th.

LV. *Seley's Bank.* Lower six inches of coal on bottom. (R. P., 1874, H, p. 160.)

The coal has a dull lustre, is hard and compact, iridescent, and contains pyrites in quantity.

Sampled August 27th. Analyzed November 4th.

LVI. *Strouse's Mine,* two and a half miles south of Reynoldsville. (R. P., 1874, H, p. 163.)

The coal is bright, shining, clean, compact, with veins of charcoal and pyrites.

Sampled September 15th. Analyzed November 27th.

	LVII.	LVIII.	LIX.	LX.
Water	1.010	1.320	1.570	1.300
Volatile matter	27.790	31.440	33.430	32.570
Fixed carbon	48.365	62.578	61.285	62.567
Sulphur	3.885	.892	1.055	1.023
Ash	18.950	3.770	2.660	2.540
	100.000	100.000	100.000	100.000
Coke, per cent	71.200	67.240	65.000	66.130
Color of Ash	Gray, pink tint.	Gray.	Brown.	Red.

LVII. *Brown's Coal Mine,* four miles south-east of Reynoldsville. (R. P., 1874, H, p. 116.)

The coal has a dull lustre, is slightly iridescent, and contains a very large amount of iron pyrites.

Sampled October 2d. Analyzed October 15th.

LVIII. *Sharp's Mine*, on Low Grade railroad, three and a half miles north-east of Reynoldsville. Upper bench. (R. P., 1874, H, p. 149.)

The coal is resinous, compact, iridescent, and contains little iron pyrites.

Sampled October 17th. Analyzed January 15th.

ANALYSES OF BITUMINOUS COALS.

LIX. *Sharp's Mine.* Lower bench. (R. P., 1874, II, p. 149.)
The coal is resinous, compact, with a coating of silt, and much pyrites.
Sampled October 17th. Analyzed January 15th.

LX. *Wachob's Mine,* four and a half miles north-west of Punxatawney. (R. P., 1874, H, p. 169.)
The coal has a dead lustre on outside; on fresh fracture a bright lustre; is strongly iridescent.
Sampled September 19th. Analyzed December 31st.

	LXI.	LXII.	LXIII.	LXIV.
Water	0.950	0.950	1.060	1.100
Volatile matter	33.550	31.590	33.200	31.170
Fixed carbon	60.523	60.520	59.428	63.544
Sulphur	1.167	1.440	2.042	1.016
Ash	3.810	5.500	4.330	3.170
	100.000	100.000	100.000	100.000
Coke, per cent	65.500	67.460	65.800	67.730
Color of Ash	Reddish brown.	Dirty Gray.	Brown, red'h tint.	Yellowish brown.

LXI. *Hawk's Mine,* two miles north-west of Punxatawney. (R. P., 1874, II, p. 171.)
The coal has a shining lustre, is hard and compact, with mineral charcoal and much iron pyrites.
Sampled September 19th. Analyzed December 30th.

LXII. *J. Thomas' Mine,* two and a half miles north of Punxatawney. (R. P., 1874, H, p. 173.)
The coal is bright, shining, compact, with many small veins of charcoal and pyrites.
Sampled September 19th. Analyzed December 31st.

LXIII. *Weaver's Mine,* three miles north, north-west of Punxatawney. (R. P., 1874, H, p. 173.)
The coal has a dull lustre, is coated with silt, friable, iridescent, with charcoal and pyrites.
Sampled September 19th. Analyzed December 23d.

LXIV. *Pantal's Mine,* four miles north-west of Punxatawney. (R. P., 1874, II, p. 176.)
The coal has a dull lustre, is hard, coated with silt, shows charcoal and pyrites, and is slightly iridescent.
Sampled September 18th. Analyzed December 30th.

	LXV.	LXVI.	LXVII.	LXVIII.
Water	1.050	1.150	0.920	1.000
Volatile matter	33.150	32.070	35.440	33.260
Fixed carbon	58.405	60.428	59.962	63.081
Sulphur	1.295	1.702	.848	1.139
Ash	6.100	4.650	2.830	1.520
	100.000	100.000	100.000	100.000
Coke, per cent	65.800	66.780	63.640	65.740
Color of Ash	Gray.	Fawn.	Brown, reddish tint.	Reddish brown.

LXV. *M'Kee's Mine*, three and a half miles north-west of Punxatawney. (R. P., 1874, H, p. 176.)

The coal is shiny, compact, somewhat slaty, with considerable iron pyrites.

Sampled September 18th. Analyzed December 29.

LXVI. *Wingert's Mine*, three miles north-west of Punxatawney. (R. P., 1874, H, p. 177.)

The coal is bright and friable, with pyrites and iron oxide.

Sampled September 18th. Analyzed December 1st.

LXVII. *Hum's Mine*, one and a half miles north-west of Punxatawney. Upper part of main bench. (R. P., 1874, H, p. 179.)

The coal is bright, with glossy lustre, compact, with a small amount of iron pyrites.

Sampled September 18th. Analyzed December 14th.

LXVIII. *Hum's Mine*. Lower part of main bench. (R. P., 1874, H, p. 179.)

The coal has a shining lustre, is somewhat compact, with a small amount of iron pyrites.

Sampled September 18th. Analyzed January 14.

	LXIX.	LXX.	LXXI.	LXXII.
Water	1.060	0.950	1.150	0.800
Volatile matter	34.140	35.870	27.705	32.020
Fixed carbon	61.172	58.218	65.835	51.887
Sulphur	.678	2.302	.930	3.593
Ash	2.950	2.660	4.380	11.700
	100.000	100.000	100.000	100.000
Coke, per cent	64.800	63.180	71.145	67.180
Color of Ash	Cream.	Red.	Red.	Gray, red tinge.

LXIX. *Ruth's Mine*, four miles west, north-west of Punxatawney. (R. P., 1874, H, p. 180.)

The coal has a dead lustre, is compact, iridescent, hard, coated with silt, and shows charcoal and pyrites.

Sampled September 18th. Analyzed December 30th.

LXX. *Anthony's Mine*, four miles west, north-west of Punxatawney. (R. P., 1874, H, p. 181.)

The coal is shining, somewhat friable, with many small veins of charcoal and pyrites.

Sampled September 18th. Analyzed December 31st.

LXXI. *London Bank*, four miles north-east of Reynoldsville. (R. P., 1874, H, p. 194.)

The coal has a dead lustre outside, bright and shining on fresh fracture, shows iridescence, and contains iron pyrites.

Sampled October 1st. Analyzed October 15th.

LXXII. Coal from bed of Sandy Creek at Reynoldsville. (R. P., 1874, H, p. 198.)

The coal is bright, shining, clean, compact, with veins of pyrites and charcoal.

Sampled September 4th. Analyzed November 14th.

	LXXIII.	LXXIV.	LXXV.	LXXVI.
Water	1.320	1.870	1.830	1.200
Volatile matter	33.920	32.450	34.270	33.630
Fixed carbon	53.905	61.103	58.353	55.796
Sulphur	1.505	.547	.767	1.504
Ash	9.350	4.030	4.780	7.870
	100.000	100.000	100.000	100.000
Coke, per cent	64.760	65.680	63.900	65.170
Color of Ash	Gray, pink tinge.	Cream.	Gray.	Gray.

LXXIII. *Wm. M'Cullough's Mine*, one and a half miles north-east of Rockdale. (R. P., 1874, H, p. 212.)

The coal has a dull lustre, is somewhat slaty, and contains much iron pyrites.

Sampled October 5th. Analyzed January 6th.

LXXIV. *S. Patten's Mine*, seven miles north, north-east of Reynoldsville. (R. P., 1874, H, p. 214.)

The coal has a dull lustre, is very friable, iridescent, with a small amount of pyrites.

Sampled October 5th. Analyzed January 8th.

LXXV. *J. J. Stewart's Mine*, eight miles north, north-east of Reynoldsville. (R. P., 1874, H, p. 215.)

The coal has a glossy lustre, is compact, and contains a small amount of iron pyrites.

Sampled October 6th. Analyzed January 7th.

LXXVI. *W. J. Calhoun's Mine*, eight and a half miles north, north-east of Reynoldsville. (R. P., 1874, H, p. 217.)

The coal is bright, shining, rather compact, with slate and iron pyrites.

Sampled October 6th. Analyzed January 8th.

	LXXVII.	LXXVIII.
Water	1.360	1.150
Volatile matter	38.720	36.000
Fixed carbon	53.683	48.099
Sulphur	2.047	7.611
Ash	4.190	7.140
	100.000	100.000
Coke, per cent	59.920	62.850
Color of Ash	Red.	Red.

LXXVII. *Key's Mine*, three-fourths of a mile west of Brockwayville. (R. P., 1874, H, p. 219.)

The coal has a glossy lustre, is rather compact, containing a small amount of iron pyrites.

Sampled October 6th. Analyzed January 7th.

LXXVIII. *P. Galusha's Mine*, Toby creek, two and a half miles north-west of Brockwayville. Second bed above iron ore. (R. P., 1874, H, p. 222.)

The coal is shining, friable, iridescent, and showing a large amount of iron pyrites. A second sample of this coal yields 8.35 per cent sulphur.

Sampled October 16th. Analyzed January 15th.

Armstrong County.

	LXXIX.	LXXX.	LXXXI.
Water	0.510	0.730	1.650
Volatile matter	30.490	31.680	39.120
Fixed carbon	46.194	49.815	52.716
Sulphur	.576	.455	2.634
Ash	22.230	17.320	3.880
	100.000	100.000	100.000
Coke, per cent	69.000	67.590	59.230
Color of Ash	Gray.	Yellow.	Brown.

LXXIX. *Red Bank Coal Company's Mine*, one and a half miles south-east of New Bethlehem. (R. P., 1874, H, p. 240.)

The coal is hard and compact, with conchoidal fracture; contains considerable carbonate of lime through it. Cannel coal. In coking, the particles do not seem to fuse together very thoroughly, and the resulting coke is only slightly coherent.

Sampled October 14th. Analyzed January 11th.

LXXX. *Red Bank Coal Company's Mine.* Second sample. (R. P., 1874, H, p. 240.)

The coal has a dull resinous lustre, is hard and compact, and contains considerable carbonate of lime. In coking, it behaves in the same way as first sample, LXXIX.

Analyzed fresh from mine.

LXXXI. *Red Bank Coal Company's Mine.* Two feet of coal under cannel. (R. P., 1874, H, p. 240.)

The coal is bright, has a resinous lustre, with considerable iron pyrites in veins.

Sampled October 14th. Analyzed January 11th.

	LXXXII.	LXXXIII.	LXXXIV
Water	1.690	1.840	1.540
Volatile matter	35.940	35.940	36.730
Fixed carbon	53.950	53.661	53.210
Sulphur	3.380	1.739	.630
Ash	5.040	6.820	7.890
	100.000	100.000	100.000
Coke, per cent	62.370	62.220	61.730
Color of Ash	Gray.	Gray.	Light yellow.

LXXXII. *Red Bank Coal Company's Mines*, one and a half miles south-east of New Bethlehem. Bed No. 2, 25 feet above cannel coal. (R. P., 1874, H, p. 241.)

The coal is bright, shining, friable, containing considerable pyrites and charcoal.

Sampled October 14th. Analyzed January 11th.

LXXXIII. *Red Bank Coal Company's Mines.* No. 3, 70 feet above cannel coal. "Orrel" coal. (R. P., 1874, H, p. 241.)

The coal is bright, very hard, with considerable iron pyrites and mineral charcoal.

Sampled October 14th. Analyzed January 11th.

LXXXIV. *Widow Thompson's Mine*, four miles south-east of New Bethlehem. (R. P., 1874, H, p. 242.)

The coal has a resinous lustre, is hard and compact, with no visible pyrites. Some of the pieces were ordinary bituminous coal, while others were decidedly cannel-like. It yields a coherent, but somewhat porous coke, having a dull lustre.

Analyzed fresh from mine.

Clarion County.

	LXXXV.	LXXXVI.	LXXXVII.
Water	1.370	1.700	1.320
Volatile matter	37.680	38.930	40.800
Fixed carbon	39.353	56.096	52.879
Sulphur	8.427	.604	.881
Ash	13.170	2.670	4.120
	100.000	100.000	100.000
Coke, per cent	60.950	59.370	58.880
Color of Ash	Red.	Cream.	Gray, with red tinge.

LXXXV. *Fairmount Coal*, on north side of Red Bank creek, one mile east of New Bethlehem. Low Grade railroad. Brookville coal from bed at railroad level. (R. P., 1874, H, p. 230.)

The coal has a dull lustre outside, resinous on fresh fracture, with pyrites, and a very large amount of sulphate of iron.

Sampled October 14th. Analyzed January 8th.

LXXXVI. *Fairmount Colliery*, on north side of Red Bank creek, one mile east of New Bethlehem. Low Grade railroad. First sample. (R. P., 1874, H, p. 231.)

The coal is bright, resinous, hard, compact, with a small amount of pyrites.

Sampled October 14th. Analyzed January 9th.

LXXXVII. *Fairmount Colliery.* Second sample. (R. P., 1874, H, p. 231.)

The coal has a dull resinous lustre, containing viens of slate and considerable pyrites.

Analyzed fresh from mine.

M'Kean County.

	LXXXVIII.	LXXXIX.	XC.
Water	1.130	1.300	1.170
Volatile matter	33.090	39.830	35.440
Fixed carbon	53.006	52.063	43.992

ANALYSES OF BITUMINOUS COALS.

	LXXXVIII.	LXXXIX.	XC.
Sulphur	1.874	1.727	1.708
Ash	10.900	5.080	17.690
	100.000	100.000	100.000
Coke, per cent	65.780	58.870	63.390
Color of Ash	Gray, with pink tint.	Yellowish white.	Gray.

LXXXVIII. Coal from three miles east of Norwich Corner. "Blue vein."

The coal has a dull lustre, somewhat coated with silt, is very hard, with pyrites, slate and charcoal.

Analyzed fresh from mine.

LXXXIX. *Lyman Mine*, near Bishop's Summit. Upper bench.

The coal has a bright resinous lustre, very hard and compact, with considerable pyrites.

Analyzed fresh from mine.

XC. *Lyman Mine.* Lower bench.

The coal has a dull lustre outside, bright on fresh fracture; very hard, strongly iridescent, with veins of slate and pyrites.

Analyzed fresh from mine.

Elk County.

	XCI.	XCII.	XCIII.
Water	2.460	2.920	1.770
Volatile matter	30.470	27.280	32.170
Fixed carbon	62.227	59.725	59.323
Sulphur	.823	.705	2.067
Ash	4.020	9.370	4.670
	100.000	100.000	100.000
Coke, per cent	67.070	69.800	66.060
Color of Ash	Cream.	Brown.	Gray, with red tinge.

XCI. *Petriken Colliery*, at Benezette. No. 1. Coal from the three foot bench. (R. P., 1874, H, p. 134.)

The coal has a shining lustre, columnar structure, containing iron pyrites.

Analyzed fresh from mine.

XCII. *Petriken Colliery.* No. 2. Coal from the two foot eight inch (top) bed. (R. P., 1874, H, p. 135.)

The coal has a dull lustre, is somewhat slaty, and containing only a little iron pyrites.

Analyzed fresh from mine.

XCIII. *Petriken Coal Opening*, at Caledonia, six miles up the creek from Benezette. No. 3. (R. P., 1874, H, p. 138.)

The coal has a dull lustre, is very friable, coated with silt, and containing considerable pyrites.

Analyzed fresh from mine.

Indiana County.

	XCIV.	XCV.
Water	1.050	1.020
Volatile matter	29.730	30.190
Fixed carbon	59.781	57.943
Sulphur	1.389	2.757
Ash	8.050	8.090
	100.000	100.000
Coke, per cent	69.220	68.790
Color of Ash	Reddish brown.	Cream.

XCIV. *G. Graff's Mine*, Canoe township, seven miles southeast of Punxatawney. (R. P., 1874, H, p. 186.)

The coal has a dirty appearance, somewhat hard, with considerable iron pyrites.

Sampled September 21st. Analyzed January 6th.

XCV. *M'Farland's Coal Mine*, Canoe township, six and a half miles east, south-east of Punxatawney. (R. P., 1874, H, p. 187.)

The coal is bright, iridescent, columnar, with considerable iron pyrites.

Sampled September 21st. Analyzed December 31st.

Blair County.

	XCVI.
Water	.700
Volatile matter	26.790
Fixed carbon	66.878
Sulphur	.802
Ash	4.830
	100.000
Coke, per cent	72.510
Color of Ash	Gray, with red tinge.

XCVI. *Tipton Coal.*

The coal has a bright shining lustre, is somewhat coated with silt, and contains much iron pyrites.

Sampled January 23d. Analyzed March 22d.

Forest County.

	XCVII.
Water	1.380
Volatile matter	36.385
Fixed carbon	38.821
Sulphur	7.714
Ash	15.700
	100.000
Coke, per cent	62.235
Color of Ash	Deep pink, nearly red.

XCVII. *Muddy Outcrop Coal*, near Marion.

The coal has a dull dirty appearance; is hard, iridescent, and contains much iron pyrites.

Sample analyzed on receipt.

ANALYSES OF COKES.

Name and locality.	Water	Volat. matter	Fixed carbon	Sulphur	Ash	Color of Ash	Description
Penn Colliery, Houtzdale, five and half miles south-west of Osceola. Coked in open air roughly	.600	2.020	88.032	.998	8.350	Red	Very hard, with silvery lustre.
Mapleton Colliery, on Shimmel's run, one and a half miles north of Osceola. Coked in open air roughly	.580	1.370	84.068	1.032	12.950	Red	Slaty, shining, iridescent.
Laurel Run Colliery, on Shimmel's run, two miles north, north-west of Osceola. Coked in open air	.510	1.300	89.243	.607	8.340	Reddish	Compact, silvery lustre.
Decatur Coal Co.'s Colliery, one and a half miles north of Philipsburg. Coked in open air	.350	2.190	90.293	.867	6.300	Red	Compact, dull gray, slaty.
Morrisdale Mine, three miles north-west of Philipsburg. Coked in open air	.250	.730	90.707	.643	7.670	Red	Compact, gray, slaty.
Snow Shoe Railroad Co.'s Colliery, Mine No. 6, Middle bed. Coked in open air from loose stuff	.990	2.950	82.626	1.104	12.330	Red	Compact, dull gray, very slaty.
Diamond (D. Reynolds) Mine, one mile north of Reynoldsville. From six foot bench of coal	.500	1.150	88.478	1.022	8.850	Cream	Hard, comp't, shining, slaty.
Hoover's Mine, (Ohio Co.) Coked from coal of six foot bench in open air	.780	1.420	88.950	.900	7.950	Reddish gray,	Comp't, slaty, & comparatively soft. Slightly iridescent.

ANALYSES OF BITUMINOUS COALS.

Phosphoric Acid in Coals.

	Per cent in Coal.	Per cent in Ash.
Penn Colliery, Houtzdale	.007	.174
Franklin Colliery, Houtzdale	.005	.047
Eureka Mine, Houtzdale	.013	.342
Stirling Mine, Houtzdale	.005	.159
Moshannon Mine, Houtzdale	.006	.162
New Moshannon Mine	.005	.124
Mapleton Colliery	.013	.253
Logan Colliery	.237	3.098
Laurel Run Colliery	.011	.366
Decatur Coal Company's Colliery	trace.	trace.
Morrisdale Mine. Lower bench	.047	1.516
Morrisdale Mine. Upper bench	.022	.830
Derby Colliery	.033	.397
Powelton Mine	trace.	trace.
William Holt's Mine. Lower hard part of bench,	.013	.273
Snow Shoe Mine, No. 4. Lower bench	.020	.191
D. Reynolds (Diamond) Mine. Upper part of six foot bed worked	trace.	trace.
Webster Mine	trace.	trace.
Hoover's Mine, (Ohio company.) Middle of six foot bench worked	.008	.166
Hoover's Mine. Upper part of six foot bench worked	.071	1.145

IRON AND SULPHUR IN COAL.

	Per ct. of sulphur,	Per cent of iron	Sulphur required by iron to form iron pyrites, (Fe S^2)	Difference	Sulphur left in coke	Per cent of sulphur in coke
Decatur Coal Co.'s Colliery. Coal from upper bench	1.373	.595	.680	.693	.842	1.118
Penn Colliery, Houtzdale	.507	.245	.280	.227	.264	.336
Franklin Colliery, Houtzdale	.875	.581	.664	.211	.328	.414
Eureka Colliery, Houtzdale	.688	.392	.448	.240	.451	.581
Mapleton Colliery, on Shimmel's run, one and a half miles north of Osceola	1.715	1.099	1.256	.459	.568	.750
Logan Colliery, on Shimmel's run, two miles north, north-west of Osceola	.867	.525	.600	.267	.628	.813
Decatur Coal Co.'s Colliery. Coal from lower bench	3.378	2.485	2.840	.538		
Morrisdale Mine, near Philipsburg	.571	.245	.280	.291	.302	.400
Powelton Mine. Lower part of bench	2.691	1.488	1.700	.991		
Seley's Bank. Bottom of six foot bench, (worked)	.736	.154	.176	.560		
Hoover's Mine, (Ohio Co.) Lower part six foot bench, (worked)	.726	.294	.336	.432		
Brown's Mine, four miles south-east of Reynoldsville	3.885	3.395	3.880	.005	2.220	3.118
Mason's Mine, one and a half miles west of Clearfield	4.232	3.780	4.320	.000	3.140	4.067
Webster Mine, five miles south-west of Osceola	.425	.189	.216	.209	.271	.354
Hum's Mine, one and a half miles north-west of Punxatawney	.848	.434	.496	.352	.390	.613
Weaver's Mine, two miles north-west of Punxatawney	2.042	1.428	1.632	.410	1.768	2.687
Mongold's Mine, four miles south-east of Troutville	2.288	1.120	1.280	1.008	.920	1.362
P. Galusha Mine, two and a half miles north-west of Brockwayville	7.611	3.570	4.080	3.531	3.456	5.498
Do .... do .... do .... 2d sample	8.350	3.590	4.100	4.250	4.510	7.158

ANALYSES OF BITUMINOUS COALS.

ANALYSES OF ASH OF COAL.

	Silica	Oxide of iron	Alumina	Lime	Magnesia	Phosphoric acid	Sulphur	Per cent. of ash in coal
Penn Colliery, Houtzdale	2.040	.350	1.140	.136	.033	.007		4.020
Eureka Mine, Houtzdale	1.660	.560	1.360	.134	.046	.013		3.800
Mapleton Colliery, one and a half miles north of Osceola	1.675	1.570	1.480	.221	.154	.013		5.130
Logan Colliery, two miles north, north-west of Osceola	3.493	.750	2.700	.302	.168	.237		7.650
Decatur Coal Company's Colliery, one and a half miles north of Philipsburg	2.100	3.550	1.550	.090	.206	trace		7.540
Morrisdale Mine, three miles north, north-west of Philipsburg	1.450	.850	.500	.200	.198	.047	.054	3.100
Powelton Mine, three miles south-east of Osceola. Lower part of bed	1.460	2.480	1.050	.180	.169	trace	.082	5.400
Seley's Bank, three miles east of Reynoldsville	1.860	.220	1.760	.060	.162			4.150
Hoover's Mine, (Ohio Co.) Reynoldsville. Lower part of six foot bench worked	1.220	.420	1.215	.120	.090	.008		3.100

REMARKS.

Water.—In glancing at the general results obtained, the exceedingly low percentage of water found in these coals is a very striking point, and in this respect they compare very favorably with the bituminous coals of other States. The average per cent of water in one hundred and forty-nine samples of Ohio coals, as shown by Prof. Wormley's analyses, is 4.65. Prof. White gives 8.57 as the average percentage of water of sixty-four samples of Iowa coals, and the analyses of Mr. Regis Chauvenet* give 3.40 as the average of one hundred and twelve specimens from Missouri. The ninety-seven samples here examined show only 1.03 as the average percentage of moisture. The hygroscopic water is not only of no advantage as combustible matter, but it actually diminishes the effective value of the fuel, as much heat is lost in transforming the water into steam and thus expelling it. The accurate determination, therefore, of the amount of moisture in a coal becomes a point of considerable importance. It was found that exposure at a temperature of 212° F. was insufficient to dry some of the coals thoroughly, so that the test was always made at 225° to 230° F. The average of sixty-six coals dried at 212° F., gave 0.786 per cent water; dried at 225° F. the average was 0.851. Many of the specimens showed a very marked difference, in one or two cases amounting to over a quarter of one per cent.

Prof. Wormley states as a singular fact, true at least of most Ohio coals, that at a temperature of 240° F., the powdered coal generally loses *less* in weight, in a given time, than at a temperature of 212°. If, therefore, a coal be thoroughly dried at 212°, and then be exposed to a heat of 240°, it will generally quickly increase in weight, due to the absorption of oxygen. This was not found to be the case with the coals I examined from this State, for in every instance was the loss greater when the coal was dried at 225° than at 212°. It is probable, therefore, that the porous, wet coals of Ohio have a greater capacity for the absorption of oxygen than the compact and comparatively dry coals of Pennsylvania. This is an interesting point when we consider the weather waste of coals. It was found that when coal was exposed to the air, it slowly parted with a considerable portion of its moisture. One sample

---

* Missouri Geological Survey, Chemical Report for 1874.

which, when freshly mined, contained 1.94 per cent water, when exposed to an ordinary temperature for one month was found to contain only 0.52 per cent, and this amount it retained, with only slight variations, due probably to the hygroscopic changes in the atmosphere, during the six months it was examined. A number of experiments would be necessary to determine this point, but the one example here given may serve as some criterion by which to judge the extent of drying the different coals have undergone by being kept in an ordinary atmosphere for several months.

Ash.—The relative amount of ash found in the bituminous coals examined, varies from 1.52 per cent, found in the coal from Hum's Mine, Jefferson county, to 19.17 per cent, existing in the coal from the upper bench (not worked) of the Diamond Colliery. The average of ash found in thirty-four coals from Clearfield county was 5.30 per cent; that of five from Centre county, 5.38 per cent. Thirty-seven coals from Jefferson county gave 5.45 per cent as the mean average of ash. In cases where excessive heat is required in the combustion of the coal, the character and quality of the ash is a point of the highest consideration. Its color affords a good indication as to its composition, a large amount of oxide of iron giving it a brown or reddish brown color. The best and most infusible are those of a white color, consisting essentially of silica and alumina, with little iron, lime or magnesia. A few analyses of the ashes have been made, which will give some idea as to their average composition.

Phosphoric acid.—It will be noticed that a small amount of phosphoric acid is invariably present. The mean average from sixteen coals gave .032 per cent phosphoric acid, which is equal to .014 per cent phosphorus. A specimen of coal from the Logan Colliery gave .237 per cent phosphoric acid, an amount fatal to this coal for use in the manufacture of Bessemer pig iron. Hitherto iron men have paid but little attention as to the freedom of their fuel from this most injurious element. In the manufacture of iron for the Bessemer process, where even a small amount of phosphorus is injurious, pure fuel becomes as much a matter of necessity as pure ores. Although the presence of phosphoric acid in the ashes of coal is a decided disadvantage to their use in the manufacture of iron, it becomes a point of the highest consideration when we view them in relation to their value for enriching impoverished tracts of land. The small amount of potash and soda we invariably find present, adds much to their value in this respect. To the farmer, therefore, the coal ashes are important, as, apart from their own intrinsic value as a fertilizer, they possess considerable absorbent powers, and may be made the vehicle for the application of liquid manures.

Volatile matter.—The amount of volatile combustible matter found in the coals examined, varies from 19.57 per cent to 40.80 per cent. The mean average of thirty-four coals from Clearfield county gave 23.64 per cent volatile combustible matter; that of five coals from Centre county, 23.81 per cent. Thirty-seven specimens from Jefferson county gave 32.60 as the mean average per cent. The average of three specimens from Clarion county gave 39.14 per cent volatile matter; that of six from Armstrong county, 34.99 per cent.

Many of the coals from Clearfield and Centre counties are known in the market as *semi-bituminous*, but their large percentage of volatile matter, as compared with standard semi-bituminous coals of the Broad Top region, entitles them to rank as *true bituminous coals.*

Fixed Carbon.—The average per cent of fixed carbon in the Clearfield county coals examined, is 68.96 per cent; that of Centre county coals 68.98 per cent, and that of Jefferson county coals 59.27 per cent.

Sulphur.—The relative amount of sulphur found in the different coals examined, varied from .425 per cent, found in the coal from the Webster colliery, to 8.427 per cent present in the coal from the lower bed of the Fairmount colliery. The mean average of the thirty-four coals from Clearfield county gave 1.36 per cent; that of five specimens from Centre county .767 per cent; that of thirty-seven from Jefferson county 1.518 per cent. Armstrong county coals gave 1.57 per cent as the average, and Clarion county coals yielded 3.30, as the mean average per cent of sulphur.

Prof. Wormley, of the Ohio State Geological Survey, has shown that many coals which contain but little iron, have yet a large percentage of sulphur. It has hitherto been supposed that the sulphur in coal existed in one of two forms, as bisulphide of iron or iron pyrites, and sulphate of lime or gypsum. Prof. Wormley's experiments, however, have proved conclusively tha a large proportion of the sulphur found in coals exists not in union with iron or lime, but as some organic compound, the exact nature of which has not been fully determined. A number of analyses made of the Pennsylvania coals for iron and sulphur, shows that the sulphur in most cases is largely in excess of the amount required to convert the iron in iron pyrites. In only two instances does all the sulphur seem to exist as bisulphide of iron. In the coal from Galusha's Mine, Jefferson county, the amount of "free sulphur," that is, the sulphur not taken up by the iron to form iron pyrites, ($Fe\ S_2$,) amounts to 3.53 per cent. This question is of equal importance to the coke manufacturer and to the manufacturer of gas, for while it is possible that the sulphur existing in the coal as iron pyrites may be partially washed out, it is scarcely probable that that portion existing as some organic compound can be got rid of in that way. The proportion of the sulphur which passes off with the volatile matter during the process of coking, seems to vary considerably. Prof. Wormley, to whom we are indebted for much valuable information on this subject, gives two instances of coals containing respectively .49 and .93 per cent of sulphur, of which there remained in the coke only .082 and .015 parts. On the other hand, another sample of coal containing .98 per cent of sulphur, of which about 90 parts existed uncombined with iron, retained .66 parts in the coke. Of the fourteen coals I examined from this State for sulphur after coking, nearly all of them were found to retain a large proportion in the coke; and in no case did the loss by coking exceed two-thirds of the sulphur originally present in the coal. In one coal, where all the sulphur, 3.88 per cent, existed as pyrites, there remained in the coke 2.22 parts, so that 1.66 parts of the sulphur passed off with the volatile matters during the process of coking. A specimen of coal from the Galusha Mine, containing 7.61 per cent of sulphur, having 3.53 parts as "free sulphur" and 4.08 parts existing as iron pyrites, lost by coking 4.15 parts of sulphur. A second sample of the Galusha coal, with 4.25 parts "free sulphur," lost by coking (the average of two experiments,) only 3.84 parts of sulphur.

It has been stated,* "that where the sulphur in coal is not combined with iron but with the volatile portion of the coal,

---

* Coal regions of America. Macfarlane, page 154.

it passes off in coking or in ordinary combustion." The single example of the Galusha coal containing 4.25 parts sulphur not combined with iron, and which lost by coking only 3.84 parts sulphur, would seem to indicate that this statement could not be made of general application. From a number of experiments made with the coals from this State, it does not appear that the sulphur, where it exists in the same coal both as pyrites and "free sulphur," passes off with the volatile matters during the process of coking, in much larger proportion than in cases where it all exists as pyrites. A large number of carefully conducted experiments will be necessary to determine what conditions are most favorable for expelling the sulphur during the process of coking.

Carbonate of lime in coal is said to have a very marked effect in retaining the sulphur in the coke, and preventing its passing off with the volatile matters during the process of coking. To the gas manufacturer, therefore, this question is one of very great importance, as it might permit the use of coals, otherwise too rich in sulphur, for the economical production of a high quality of illuminating gas.

In order to test the point, the following experiments were made. A coal, rich in sulphur, was coked in a platina crucible in the usual way, and the amount of sulphur left in the coke estimated. The same coal was then coked with the addition of a certain percentage of carbonate of lime, and the sulphur estimated in the resulting coke. It may be stated as an interesting point, that the coke produced by coking the coal with carbonate of lime, gave off a strong odor of sulphuretted hydrogen gas, whereas the coke produced from the same coal without the addition of carbonate of lime, gave no smell of sulphuretted hydrogen. The results of the experiments are embodied in the following table:

Sulphur in coal = 8.35 per cent.	Coked with 5 per cent carbonate of lime	Cok'd with 10 pr. cent carbonate of lime	Coked with 5 per cent lime	Coked with no addition	Coked with no addition
Sulphur left in coke	4.846	5.046	5.611	4.537	4.488

The Weather Waste of Coal.

The changes which a coal undergoes by exposure to the [we]ather, is a question of equal importance to the miner and to [th]e consumer of coal. It has generally been supposed that bitu[mi]nous coals part with a large amount of their volatile com[bu]stible matter, and otherwise deteriorate very much in quality [by] exposure to the weather. This waste depends on their power [to] absorb oxygen, causing the coal to undergo a slow combustion, [co]nverting the hydro-carbons into water and carbonic acid. [Th]e presence of moisture is also said to be an important condi[tio]n. Mr. Richard P. Rothwell, M. E., in an article on "Ala[ba]ma coal and iron,"* gives us the following points in regard [to] the weather waste of different coals : * * * "It is [s]o essential that the coal be freshly mined, for experiments [ha]ve been made that show that the deterioration which a coal [un]dergoes by even a very limited exposure to the atmosphere [is] quite considerable. For example : According to Dr. Richter, [th]e weather waste of a coal depends on its ability to absorb [ox]ygen, converting the hydro-carbons into water and carbonic [ac]id. Grundman found that coal exposed for nine months to [th]e atmosphere, lost 50 cent of its value as a fuel. He states [th]at the decomposition takes place in the middle of a heap the [sa]me as at the surface, and it reached its maximum about the [th]ird or fourth week ; and one-half the oxygen was absorbed [du]ring the first fourteen days. He also found that a coal poor [in] oxygen absorbs it most rapidly, and that the presence of [m]oisture is an important condition. Coal which made, when [fr]eshly mined, a good compact coke, after eleven days exposure [ei]ther would not coke at all, or it made an inferior coke. For [ga]s purposes the coal is also greatly injured by the loss of its [vo]latile hydro-carbons.

"Varrentrapp, of Brunswick, found in his experiments that [ox]idation of the coal takes place even at common temperature, [w]here moisture is present. Coal exposed to a temperature of [8]4° Fah. for three months lost all its hydro-carbons, a fact [w]hich shows that the conversion of bituminous coal into an[t]racite was not necessarily accompanied by a high temperature.

* The Engineering and Mining Journal, Vol. XVII, No. 4, page 51. 1874.

He found also that the weather waste in some cases amounted to 33 per cent, and in one instance the gas yielding quality decreased 45 per cent, and the heating power 47 per cent, while the same coal under cover lost in the same time but 24 per cent for gas purposes, and 12 per cent for fuel.

The harder varieties of bituminous coal, such for example as the cannel and splint coals of West Virginia, Ohio and Indiana, do not appear to lose much by exposure to the atmosphere, except it be in heaps of slack where the conditions are favorable for the generation of a high temperature. Anthracite appears to be still less affected by exposure, for the fine coal which has lain for the past twenty years in our culm banks, exposed to the rain, and under conditions the most favorable for decomposition, being mixed with shales containing a large amount of iron pyrites, which in decomposing generate a very high temperature in the whole mass, is yet found to burn well, almost as well as that freshly mined, while the large lump coal has been used in our blast furnaces after an exposure of twelve years, and no perceptible difference in its quality could be noticed. It is nevertheless quite certain that most varieties of bituminous coal deteriorate very rapidly and to an extent but little appreciated. These important results should be borne in mind, not only in providing for the storage of coal, but also in selecting samples for analysis.'

Sufficient time has not been allowed during the present survey to collect the mass of facts necessary for a proper discussion of the coals of this State as to their weather waste, but the few analyses already made are given underneath in the hope that they may serve to throw some light on this interesting subject, and at the same time show that the general impression that all bituminous coals lose part of their volatile combustible matter by exposure to the weather, does not hold good at least in so far as the compact and dry bituminous coals of Pennsylvania are concerned.

The German Railway Association have had different coals exposed to the weather for twelve months and then re-examined, and the results of their experiments are here added for the sake of comparison.

ANALYSES OF BITUMINOUS COALS.

Weather waste in Coal.

BITUMINOUS COAL FROM THE FRANKLIN COLLIERY.	Freshly mined coal.	After being weathered for six months.
Water	1.942	1.060
Volatile matter	22.720	22.700
Fixed carbon	71.018	72.075
Sulphur	.553	.515
Ash	3.777	3.650
	100.000	100.000
Coke, per cent	75.340	76.240

BITUMINOUS COAL.	APRIL. Freshly mined coal.	MAY. Covered.	MAY. Weathered	JUNE. Covered.	JUNE. Weathered
Water	1.942	.520	.965	.590	.700
Volatile matter	22.720	22.830	21.715	22.830	22.450
Fixed Carbon	71.561	72.770	73.880	72.020	72.650
Ash	3.777	3.880	3.440	4.560	4.200
	100.000	100.000	100.000	100.000	100.000
Coke, per cent	75.340	76.650	77.320	76.580	76.850

BITUMINOUS COAL.	JULY. Covered.	JULY. Weathered	AUGUST. Weathered	SEPTEM'R. Weathered
Water	.565	.935	.780	1.060
Volatile matter	23.090	22.560	22.980	22.700
Fixed carbon	71.989	72.455	72.300	72.590
Ash	4.356	4.050	3.940	3.650
	100.000	100.000	100.000	100.000
Coke, per cent	76.350	76.510	76.240	76.240

GAS COAL.	Freshly mined.	After exposure for 3 months.
Water	1.030	.81
Volatile matter	38.230	38.52
Fixed carbon	52.561	52.35
Sulphur	1.709	1.69
Ash	6.470	6.63
	100.000	100.00
Coke, per cent	60.740	60.67

GAS COAL.	JULY. Freshly mined.	AUGUST. Weather'd.	SEPT. Weather'd
Water	1.030	.760	.81
Volatile matter	38.230	38.017	38.52
Fixed carbon	54.270	54.403	54.04
Ash	6.470	6.820	6.63
	100.000	100.000	100.00
Coke, per cent	60.740	61.220	60.67

German Railway Association's Experiments.

After exposure of the coals for twelve months, the following losses were determined. NAME OF COAL.	Weight per cent.	Caloric per cent.	Yield of coke per ct
Pease's West Hartley, coking	0.0	0.0	0.
Glucksburg seam, Ibbenbüren	1.4	6.0	4.
Carl Mine, near Dortmund	....	2.6	2.
Hibernia Mine, Gelsenkirchen	0.4	0.6	2.
Constantin Mine, Bochum	0.4	0.4	0.
Borgloke Mine, Osnabrück	2.0	6.0	0.

By glancing at the tables given above, it will be seen that the coals tested have not changed materially in their chemical composition, even after an exposure of several months. Weathering the coal may have a very decided effect in eliminating the sulphur. A quantity of coal containing 1.86 per cent of sulphur, existing chiefly as iron pyrites, was put into a glass funnel, the neck of which was loosely filled with pieces of glass and exposed to the action of the weather for several weeks. The funnel was so arranged that the rain water filtering through the coal was collected in a glass beaker underneath. On examination of the solution it was found to contain considerable ferrous and ferric salts, with quite a large amount of sulphuric acid.

The decomposition of the pyrites in coal is attended by the generation of considerable heat which will have the effect of disintegrating the coal, unfitting it for bearing transportation equally well. This question will be an important one in considering the weather waste of coals in all its bearings. A long series of experiments will be necessary to determine under what conditions oxidation of the coal takes place most readily. It is probable that porous, spongy coals having a large percentage of water, may also possess a greater capacity for the absorption of oxygen, and consequent weather waste.

No attempt has been made at a discussion of the different coals as to their steam raising powers, but as their chemical composition bears some relation to their heat producing qualities, the analyses given in the preceding pages are here grouped together for convenience of comparison, followed by a condensed table taken from Prof. Johnson's elaborate experiments to the U. S. Navy Department.

COALS

NAME OF COLLIERY.	Water	Volatile matter	Fixed carbon	Sulphur	Ash	Color of Ash.	Coke, per cent.
Clearfield County.							
1. Penn Colliery	.810	20.640	74.023	.507	4.020	White	78.550
2. Franklin Colliery	1.942	22.720	71.018	.543	3.777	Cream	75.340
3. Eureka Mine	.780	21.680	73.052	.688	3.800	Gray	77.540
4. Stirling Mine	.710	23.400	72.218	.532	3.140	Gray, with red tinge	75.890
5. Moshannon Colliery	.765	20.090	74.779	.666	3.700	...do......do.....	79.145
6. New Moshannon Mine	1.100	23.070	71.199	.611	4.020	Red	75.830
7. Hale's Colliery. Upper bed	.570	24.630	68.400	1.900	4.500	Gray, with red tinge.	74.800
8. Hale's Colliery. Lower bed	.740	25.210	68.628	2.122	3.300	Red	74.050
9. Mapleton Colliery	.700	23.565	68.890	1.715	5.130	Gray	75.735
10. Logan Colliery	.620	22.135	68.728	.867	7.650	Gray	77.245
11. Laurel Run Colliery	.800	23.260	72.350	.590	3.000	Red	75.940
12. Decatur Coal Co.'s Colliery. Lower bench	.640	21.360	64.082	3.378	7.540	Gray, with red tinge.	75.000
13. Decatur Coal Co.'s Colliery. Upper bench	.820	23.900	69.007	1.373	4.900	...do......do.....	75.280
14. Morrisdale Mine. Lower bench	.550	24.090	71.689	.571	3.100	Gray	75.360
15. Morrisdale Mine. Upper bench	.560	25.190	71.013	.587	2.650	Salmon	74.250
16. Derby Colliery	.410	22.810	66.690	1.790	8.300	Gray, with red tinge	76.780
17. Reitur's Colliery. Upper bed	.630	24.630	70.396	.654	3.690	Red	74.740
18. Mon's Mine	.750	19.570	69.833	.677	9.170	Gray, with red tinge	79.680
19. Hill's Mine	.380	22.280	67.995	2.455	6.890	Dirty gray, with red tinge,	77.340
20. Humphrey's Mine	.410	21.800	72.903	1.087	3.800	Red	77.790
21. Mason's Mine. Upper bench	.550	22.650	72.616	1.334	2.850	Red	76.800
22. Mason's Mine. Lower bench	.480	22.320	59.788	4.232	13.180	Pinkish	77.200
23. G. W. Davis' Mine	.640	23.010	71.799	.551	4.000	Red	76.350
24. Jeremiah Cooper's Mine	.700	24.020	64.951	1.639	8.690	Red	75.280
25. Williamson's Mine	.620	22.730	68.794	1.576	6.280	Gray	76.650
26. Powelton Mine. Lower part of bed	.600	22.600	68.709	2.691	5.400	Gray, with pink tinge.	76.800
27. Powelton Mine. Upper part of bed	.540	22.500	71.551	1.079	4.270	Light gray	76.900

ANALYSES OF BITUMINOUS COALS. M. 39

28.	Webster Colliery	1.630	22.000	72.815	.425	3.130	Gray, with slight red tinge	76.370
29.	Bell's Mine	.950	32.450	59.904	1.296	5.400	Gray	66.600
30.	Tyler's Mine	.940	31.060	61.563	1.487	4.950	Gray, with red tinge	68.000
31.	R. Shaw's Mine	.870	21.680	68.928	1.302	7.220	Pinkish	77.450
32.	J. Shaw's Mine	.520	21.030	67.133	.767	10.550	Reddish gray	78.450
33.	Mongold's Mine	.860	31.600	61.662	2.228	3.590	Brown	67.540
34.	Hubler's Mine	.420	25.010	67.221	2.479	4.870	Pink	74.570

Centre County.

1.	Snow Shoe Mines. Upper bed. Mine No. 5	1.280	25.580	68.937	.613	3.590	Cream	73.140
2.	Snow Shoe Mines. Middle bed. Mine No. 6	.650	24.560	70.416	.964	3.410	Cream	74.790
3.	Snow Shoe Mines. Lower bed (B). Mine No. 4	.750	23.440	64.374	.986	10.450	Gray, with red tinge	76.800
4.	Wm. Holt's Mine, west of Holt's Hill	.880	23.620	70.089	.661	4.750	Red	75.500
5.	Wm. Holt's Mine, Snow Shoe basin. Upper b'h	1.680	21.870	71.108	.612	4.730	Red	76.450

Jefferson County.

1.	Seley's Bank. Upper bench	.850	31.200	59.882	1.368	6.700	Dirty gray, with red tinge	67.950
2.	Seley's Bank. Middle bench	1.040	31.610	62.464	.736	4.150	Gray, with red tinge	67.350
3.	Seley's Bank. Lower bench	.960	32.320	58.640	1.230	6.850	Gray, with pink tinge	66.720
4.	Shiesley's Bank. Upper bench	1.600	30.700	63.791	.639	3.270	Red	67.700
5.	Shiesley's Bank. Lower bench	1.480	29.220	65.022	.608	3.670	Gray, with red tinge	69.300
6.	Diamond Colliery. Upper bench ... not	1.100	29.990	46.639	3.101	19.170	...do ...do...	68.910
7.	Diamond Colliery. Middle bench.. } worked {	1.190	32.810	55.816	2.284	8.400	Gray, with pink tinge	66.000
8.	Diamond Colliery. Mid. port'n	.950	35.130	59.304	1.436	3.180	Dirty gray	63.920
9.	Diamond Colliery. Lower bench. Low. por'n	1.120	33.860	60.692	1.278	3.050	Gray, with red tinge	65.020
10.	Hoover Bank. Upper bench	.960	32.680	59.097	1.063	6.200	...do ...do...	66.360
11.	Hoover Bank. Middle bench	1.100	30.800	62.524	.776	4.800	Cream	68.100
12.	Hoover Bank. Lower bench	1.100	32.900	62.174	.726	3.100	Cream	66.000
13.	Sprague's Mine	1.430	31.940	62.109	.531	3.990	Cream	66.630
14.	Wachob's Mine	1.300	32.570	62.567	1.023	2.540	Red	66.130
15.	J. Thomas' Mine	.950	31.590	60.520	1.440	5.500	Dirty gray	67.460
16.	Anthony's Mine	.950	35.870	58.218	2.302	2.660	Red	63.180
17.	P. Hawk's Mine	.950	33.550	60.523	1.167	3.810	Reddish brown	65.500
18.	Ruth's Mine	1.060	34.140	61.172	.678	2.950	Cream	64.800
19.	Pantall's Mine	1.100	31.170	63.544	1.016	3.170	Yellowish brown	67.730
20.	M'Kee's Mine	1.050	33.150	58.405	1.295	6.100	Gray	65.800
21.	Weaver's Mine	1.000	33.200	59.428	2.042	4.330	Brown, red tinge	65.800
22.	Wingert's Mine	1.150	32.070	60.428	1.702	4.650	Fawn	66.780
23.	Hum's Mine. Upper bench	.920	35.440	59.962	.848	2.830	Brown	63.640

COALS—Continued.

NAME OF COLLIERY.	Water.	Volatile matter.	Fixed carbon.	Sulphur.	Ash.	Color of Ash.	Coke, per cent.
Jefferson County—Continued.							
24. Hum's Mine. Lower bench	1.000	33.260	63.081	1.139	1.520	Brown	65.740
25. W. Reynolds' Mine	1.440	32.460	63.011	.639	2.450	Cream	66.100
26. Sharp's Mine. Upper bench	1.320	31.440	62.578	.892	3.770	Gray	67.240
27. Sharp's Mine. Lower bench	1.570	33.430	61.285	1.055	2.660	Brown	65.000
28. London Mine	1.150	27.705	65.835	.930	4.380	Red	71.140
29. Strouse's Mine	1.300	30.220	63.617	.763	4.100	Lavender	68.480
30. Creek, Reynoldsville	.800	32.020	51.887	3.593	11.700	Gray, with red tinge	67.180
31. Brown's Mine	1.010	27.790	48.365	3.885	18.950	Gray, with pink tinge	71.200
32. Wm. M'Cullough's Mine	1.320	33.920	53.905	1.505	9.350	....do....	64.760
33. S. Patten's Mine	1.870	32.450	61.103	.547	4.030	Cream	65.680
34. J. Stewart's Mine	1.880	34.270	58.353	.767	4.780	Gray	63.900
35. J. Calhoun's Mine	1.200	33.630	55.796	1.504	7.870	Gray	65.170
36. Key's Mine	1.360	38.720	53.683	2.047	4.190	Red	59.920
37. P. Galusha's Mine	1.150	36.000	48.099	7.611	7.140	Red	62.850
Armstrong County.							
1. Red Bank Colliery. Cannel	.510	30.490	46.194	.576	22.230	Gray	69.000
2. Red Bank Colliery. Cannel	.730	31.680	48.815	.455	17.320	Yellow	67.590
3. Red Bank Colliery. Below Cannel	1.650	39.120	52.716	2.634	3.880	Brown	59.230
4. Red Bank Colliery. Middle bed	1.690	35.944	53.950	3.380	5.040	Gray	62.870
5. Red Bank Colliery. Upper bed	1.840	35.940	53.661	1.739	6.820	Gray	62.220
6. Thompson's Mine	1.540	36.730	53.210	.630	7.890	Light yellow	61.730
Clarion County.							
1. Fairmount. Big bed	1.320	40.800	52.879	.881	4.120	Gray, with red tinge	58.880
2. Fairmount. Big bed	1.700	38.930	56.096	.604	2.670	Cream	59.370
3. Fairmount. Lower bed	1.370	37.680	39.353	8.427	13.170	Red	60.950

ANALYSES OF BITUMINOUS COALS. M. 41

STEAM RAISING POWER OF COALS.

Results of United States Government experiments in burning coal under a steam boiler.

NAMES OF COALS IN THE ORDER OF EVAPORATIVE POWER UNDER EQUAL BULKS.	Water	Volatile matter	Fixed carbon	Sulphur	Ash	Coke	Pounds of steam from 212° produced by 1 cubic foot of each coal	Pounds of steam produced from water at 212° by 1 lb of fuel	Relative evaporative power for equal bulks of coal
		COMPOSITION IN 100 PARTS.					EFFICIENCY.		
1. Atkinson & Templeman's	.446	15.532	75.688		7.334	84.022	566.2	10.700	1.000
2. Beaver Meadow. Slope, No. 5	.892	3.604	90.355	0.062	5.149	95.504	556.1	9.880	.982
3. Peach Mountain	1.897	2.958	89.020	0.006	6.125	95.145	545.7	10.110	.964
4. Forest Improvement	1.785	3.050	90.751	0.016	4.414	95.165	540.8	10.060	.955
5. Easby's "Coal in Store"	.649	14.984	76.264		8.083	84.347	535.6	10.020	.946
6. New York and Maryland Mining Company	1.785	12.309	73.503		12.403	85.903	524.8	9.780	.927
7. Quin's Run	.836	17.868	72.787	.102	8.406	81.193	517.0	10.270	.913
8. Blossburg	1.339	13.927	73.103	.853	10.773	83.881	515.9	9.720	.911
9. Neff's, Cumberland	2.455	12.675	74.527		10.343	84.870	512.7	9.440	.906
10. Easby & Smith's	.893	15.522	74.289		9.296	83.585	511.1	9.960	.903
11. Beaver Meadow. Slope, No. 3	1.562	2.384	88.942	0.011	7.112	96.052	505.5	9.210	.893
12. Beaver Meadow. (Navy Yard)					8.104		500.4	9.080	.883
13. Mixture, 1-5th Cumberland, 4-5ths Beaver Meadow					8.176		498.5	9.180	.880
14. Lehigh	0.000	5.285	89.153	.030	5.562	94.715	494.0	8.930	.872
15. Lycoming Creek	.670	13.807	71.532		13.961	85.493	493.3	8.910	.871
16. Cambria County	2.455	19.019	69.373	1.500	9.153	78.526	486.9	9.240	.869
17. Mixture, 1-5th Midlothian, 4-5ths Beaver Meadow					8.885		481.1	8.830	.859
18. Barr's Deep Run	1.785	19.782	67.958		10.475	78.433	478.7	9.020	.845
19. Lackawanna	2.120	3.793	87.741	0.123	6.346	94.087	477.7	9.790	.844

STEAM RAISING POWER OF COALS—Continued.

NAMES OF COALS IN THE ORDER OF EVAPORATIVE POWER UNDER EQUAL BULKS.	COMPOSITION IN 100 PARTS.						EFFICIENCY.		
	Water	Volatile matter	Fixed carbon	Sulphur	Ash	Coke	Pounds of steam from 212° produced by 1 cubic foot of each coal	Pounds of steam produced from water at 212° by 1 ℔ of fuel	Relative evaporative power for equal bulks of coal
20. Karthaus	1.282	17.948	73.770	1.580	7.000	80.770	477.4	9.090	.843
21. Dauphin and Susquehanna	.446	13.547	74.244	.269	11.494	85.738	472.8	9.340	.835
22. Lykens Valley	0.111	6.796	83.841	0.091	9.252	93.093	459.7	9.460	.812
23. Pictou, (New York)	2.567	27.063	56.981	.769	13.389	70.370	450.6	8.410	.796
24. Midlothian, (average)	2.455	29.796	53.012	.058	14.737	67.749	448.5	8.290	.792
25. Crouch & Snead's	1.785	23.959	59.976	.427	14.280	74.256	445.0	8.340	.786
26. New Castle	2.007	35.597	56.996	.230	5.400	62.396	439.6	8.660	.776
27. Midlothian, (900 feet shaft)	1.172	27.278	61.083		10.467	71.550	433.7	8.580	.766
28. Midlothian, "New Shaft"	.670	33.490	56.400	2.286	9.440	65.840	418.6	8.750	.739
29. Pictou, (Cunard's)	.781	25.975	60.735		12.508	73.243	417.9	8.480	.738
30. Chesterfield Mining Company	1.896	30.676	58.794	1.957	8.634	67.428	410.9	9.000	.726
31. Midlothian, (screened)	1.785	34.497	54.063	.202	9.655	63.718	408.7	8.940	.722
32. Natural Coke	1.116	11.977	75.081	.466	11.826	86.907	395.3	8.470	.698
33. Creek Company's	1.450	29.678	60.300	2.890	8.572	68.872	391.8	8.420	.692
34. Pittsburg	1.397	36.603	54.926	.160	7.074	62.000	384.1	8.200	.678
35. Sidney	3.125	23.810	67.570		5.495	73.065	378.9	7.990	.669
36. Liverpool	.892	39.587	54.899	.376	4.622	59.521	375.4	7.840	.663
37. Scotch	3.013	38.837	48.812	.358	9.338	58.150	353.8	6.950	.625
38. Tippecanoe	1.841	34.165	54.620	.377	9.374	63.994	350.2	7.750	.618
39. Cannelton, (Ia.)	2.597	33.992	58.437		4.974	63.411	348.8	7.340	.616
40. Clover Hill	1.339	31.698	56.831	.514	10.132	66.963	347.7	7.670	.614

CHAPTER II.

(*Section* 1.)

IRON ORES.

Method of Analysis.

1. *Water.*—A weighed quantity of the ore is heated in a glass bulb, to which is attached a counterpoised chloride of calcium tube. By this operation the water is driven off and collected in the chloride of calcium tube, the increase in weight of which gives the amount of water present in the ore.

It may be here stated that all the ores were dried at 100° *C. previous to analysis, so that the amount of water given in any analysis represents that portion only which exists in chemical combination in the ore.*

2. *Sulphuric Acid.*—A weighed quantity of the ore, in fine powder, is dissolved in hydrochloric acid and the solution evaporated to dryness; re-dissolved in dilute acid, and the insoluble residue filtered off. The sulphuric acid in the filtrate is then precipitated by means of chloride of barium, and the solution is allowed to stand over for twelve hours. It is best to have the solution hot and only slightly acid previous to precipitation of the sulphur. From the weight of the sulphate of baryta obtained the percentage of sulphuric acid is calculated.

In cases where the sulphur exists as pyrites, the ore is dissolved in nitric acid with the addition of a small amount of hydrochloric acid, and treated as before. When a large amount of pyrites is present, it is much better to fuse the finely pulverized ore with carbonate of soda and nitrate of potash, dissolve the fused mass in water, acidulate with hydrochloric acid, and evaporate to dryness so as to get rid of all nitric acid. The residue is then dissolved in dilute acid, the insoluble matter filtered off, and the sulphuric acid precipitated with chloride of barium.

3. *Phosphoric Acid.*—Five grammes of the finely pulverized ore are dissolved in aqua regia and the solution evaporated com-

pletely to dryness; re-dissolved in dilute hydrochloric acid, and the insoluble residue separated by filtration. The iron in the solution is now reduced to the state of proto-chloride by means of sulphite of ammonia, and the solution boiled to expel any excess of sulphurous acid that may have been used. A small portion of the iron is then oxidized by means of chlorate of potash, the solution nearly neutralized with ammonia, and the phosphoric acid precipitated as phosphate of iron by means of acetate of ammonia. The solution is then boiled for some minutes, the precipitate filtered off, washed well with hot water, and then dissolved in hydrochloric acid. This solution is now evaporated down to a small bulk, and just enough citric acid added to prevent the iron from being thrown down by ammonia. The liquid is now made strongly alkaline by means of ammonia, and after the solution has cooled, "magnesia mixture" is added, which throws down the phosphoric acid as ammonio phosphate of magnesium. The solution is stirred vigorously and allowed to stand aside for sixteen hours, so as to ensure the complete precipitation of all the phosphoric acid. The precipitate is then filtered off, washed with ammonia water, dried, ignited carefully, and weighed. From the weight of the pyro-phosphate of magnesia obtained the percentage of phosphoric acid is readily calculated.

4. *Insoluble residue.*—One gramme of the ore, in fine powder, is digested in strong hydrochloric acid until no further action takes place. The solution is then evaporated cautiously to dryness; re-dissolved in dilute hydrochloric acid, and filtered. The insoluble residue which remains is well washed with hot water, and in order to dissolve the iron thoroughly out of the filter a little dilute acid is added, after which the washing is continued until the wash water is no longer acid. The filter and contents are then ignited in a platina crucible and the weight of the insoluble residue noted.

When it becomes necessary to analyze this residue the method of analysis as given for fire-clays may be used.

5. *Manganese.*—The filtrate and washings from the insoluble residue are nearly neutralized with ammonia, heated to the boiling point, and the iron, alumina, &c., thrown down by means of a *slight* excess of acetate of ammonia. The solution

is then boiled thoroughly, and filtered while still hot. This precipitation is repeated, so as to ensure the complete separation of the last traces of manganese. Preserve the precipitate for the estimation of the iron and alumina. The filtrates are now evaporated down to a small bulk, transferred to a flask, and the solution rendered slightly alkaline with ammonia. A few drops of bromine are then added, the mixture agitated so as to aid separation, and the flask, after being tightly corked, is allowed to stand aside for twelve hours. The solution is then boiled and the precipitated oxide of manganese separated by filtration. This precipitate is now dissolved in hydrochloric acid, and the manganese thrown down from the solution by means of carbonate of soda. Filter off the precipitate, wash well with hot water, and afterwards dry, ignite and weigh. From the weight of the ignited oxide (Mn_3O_4) the metallic manganese is readily calculated.

6. *Lime.*—The filtrate from the precipitation of the oxide of manganese by means of bromine, is treated with oxalate of ammonia, which throws down the lime as oxalate. The solution is allowed to stand over for some time, after which the oxalate of lime is filtered off, washed, dried and ignited; the resulting carbonate of lime is then converted into sulphate by the addition of a small amount of sulphuric acid, having previously dissolved the carbonate in a small quantity of dilute hydrochloric acid. Excess of alcohol is then added, and the mixture set aside for twelve hours. The lime is weighed as sulphate, and its percentage calculated therefrom.

7. *Magnesia.*—The filtrate from the oxalate of lime is made strongly alkaline by means of ammonia, and the magnesia thrown down with phosphate of soda. The solution is allowed to stand aside for twelve hours, after which the phosphate of magnesia is filtered off, washed with ammonia water, ignited and weighed. From the weight of the phosphate ($2\,MgO, PO_5$) obtained the per cent of magnesia is calculated.

8. *Alumina and Iron.*—The precipitate produced in the hydrochloric acid solution of the ore by means of acetate of ammonia, (5) is dissolved in hydrochloric acid and precipitated with ammonia, filtered off, and washed well with hot water. This gives the iron, alumina and phosphoric acid. The precipitate

after being ignited and weighed, is dissolved in the hydrochloric acid, and the iron estimated by means of a standard solution of bichromate of potash. By deducting the oxide of iron and phosphoric acid from the total weight of the oxides found in the previous experiment, the amount of alumina is obtained. Estimation by "difference" is generally objectionable, but the separation of iron and alumina, *where the iron is largely in excess*, by means of caustic potash is so unsatisfactory that the above method is used in preference.

9. *Iron.*—A separate estimation of iron is always made from the ore direct. For this purpose, the volumetric process, first suggested by Dr. Penny, is very convenient and gives excellent results. It is based on the fact that when bichromate of potash, dissolved in water, is added to an acid solution of a protosalt of iron, the latter is converted into a persalt at the expense of the oxygen of the chromic acid. An indirect method is necessary to ascertain when the reaction is finished, and for this purpose a weak solution of ferricyanide of potassium (red prussiate of potash) is used, which produces a blue or bluish-green color with the protosalts of iron, but is unaltered by the persalts of that metal.

The standard solution is readily prepared by dissolving thirty-six grammes of the pure crystallized bichromate of potassium, previously freed from hygroscopic water by heating to incipient fusion, in eight litres of distilled water; of this solution about 200 c. c. will be equivalent to one gramme of metallic iron. The strength of the solution is readily ascertained by dissolving 0.5 gramme pure iron wire in dilute hydrochloric acid, taking care that no oxidation takes place, diluting the solution with distilled water, and adding the bichromate of potash from a burette until a drop no longer gives the slightest trace of a bluish-green color when transferred, by a glass rod, to a white porcelain slab wetted with the solution of ferricyanide of potassium.

The solution may be made of any strength, but one of which every c. c. represents 0.25 to 0.50 per cent iron, will be found most convenient for general use in the estimation of iron in ordinary iron ores.

For ores, the method is as follows: One gramme of the finely pulverized ore is heated with strong hydrochloric acid until solution is complete. It is now diluted with distilled water, and the per-chloride of iron reduced to the state of proto-chloride by means of zinc. The standard solution of bichromate of potash is now added from a burette, and the operation conducted as given above in the preparation of the standard solution.

10. *Titanic Acid.*—When titanic acid is present, the ore is decomposed by fusing with twelve times its weight of bisulphate of soda, dissolving the fused mass in cold water, filtering off the silica, and precipitating the titanic acid in the solution by continued boiling.

11. *Carbonic Acid.*—This is most readily determined by the use of Rose's carbonic acid apparatus, the weight of the charged apparatus being carefully ascertained, and its weight again determined after the complete expulsion of the carbonic acid.

Notes.—When the gangue of an ore is of such a nature that solution in hydrochloric acid fails to represent the true character of the specimen, decomposition is effected by fusing the finely pulverized ore with carbonate of soda, dissolving in water, acidulating with hydrochloric acid, evaporating to dryness, and treating the residue in the usual way. Such analyses are recognized in these tables by showing the percentage of *silica* instead of *insoluble residue.*

Where metals of unusual occurrence are present, special methods have to be adopted for their separation and estimation, but it is believed that the above processes are sufficient for the general run of ores. The number of analyses required by the different Assistant Geologists has been so great that a complete analysis of each sample has been impossible. An endeavor has been made, however, to make the examination complete enough so as to represent the true character of the specimen.

In the case of *brown hematite ores*, the percentage of iron, manganese, sulphur, phosphorus and insoluble residue is given; the undetermined portion consisting essentially of water of combination, alumina, lime, magnesia, and oxygen in union with the bases &c., estimated.

In *carbonate ores*, the residue consists chiefly of alumina, lime, magnesia, organic matter, water, and a large amount of carbonic acid in union with the bases.

The samples sent in to the Laboratory varied very much in quantity; in most cases, however, they were sufficient to fairly represent the average of the mine. This is especially the case with those sent in by Prof. Persifor Frazer, Jr., from York county, the average sample being about two hundred and fifty pounds of the ore.

Section 2.

Brown Hematite Ores, Silurian, Lehigh County.

The number of brown hematite ores examined from Lehigh county is thirty-eight.

The percentage of iron found varies from 28.10 to 58.50 per cent. The mean average per cent is 46.09. The amount of sulphur present is invariably very small; the average percentage being only 0.025.

The per cent of phosphorus varies from 3.135, found in the ore from Jacob Steininger's Mine, to 0.025, present in the ore from Frank S. Lichtenwalner's Mine. The mean average per cent of the thirty-eight samples examined is 0.344.

The insoluble residue gives as the mean average 17.16 per cent.

The amount of manganese varies from a trace to 9.28 per cent. The mean average per cent is 1.275.

These ores are used for the most part in the furnaces situated in the Lehigh valley, and are smelted usually with the compact magnetites from New Jersey. The product is said to be a good quality of foundry iron. The fuel used is anthracite, with hot blast. The ores are invariably used raw. The percentage of phosphorus is generally too large to admit of their extensive use in the manufacture of Bessemer pig iron, but many of them might be used for this purpose in connection with the more compact but less phosphoric magnetic iron ores.

	I.	II.	III.	IV.
Iron	37.000	32.700	46.600	45.300
Manganese	3.033	.374	.454	.749
Sulphur	.035	.030	.027	.032
Phosphorus	.186	.179	.597	.137
Insoluble residue	28.990	39.050	16.230	21.060

I. *Harry Kaiser's Mine*, leased by Mull and Hagenbuch,

ANALYSES OF IRON ORES. M. 49

north of Lock Ridge, one mile west of Alburtis. (R. P., 1874, D, p. 18.)

Sample partly lump and partly fine ore.

Limonite, hard and sandy, with considerable quartz in fine ore.

II. *Jonas Kreischmann's Mine*, leased by Allentown Rolling Mill Company, one mile east of Alburtis. Vein ore. (R. P., 1874, D, p. 18.)

Limonite, hard, compact and very sandy.

III. *Jonas Kreischmann's Mine*, leased by Coleraine Iron Company, one mile east of Alburtis. Wash ore. (R. P., 1874, D, p. 19.)

Limonite, wash ore, with considerable admixture of ferruginous clay.

IV. *Wiand's Mine*, leased by the Temple Iron Company. (R. P., 1874, D, p. 21.)

Sandy limonite, with considerable quartz in the fine ore

	V.	VI.	VII.	VIII.
Iron	46.500	33.300	47.000	47.900
Manganese	.590	.612	.518	.266
Sulphur	.022	.007	.030	.003
Phosphorus	.128	.170	.111	.165
Insoluble residue	16.300	34.250	16.050	11.890

V. *P. Marck's Mine*, leased by Lehigh Iron Company. (R. P., 1874, D. p. 21.)

Limonite, hard, compact, arenaceous, with somewhat slaty structure.

VI. *Maple Grove Mill* property near Hensingerville. (R. P., 1874, D, p. 21.)

Limonite, hard, compact, exceedingly silicious, with slaty structure, and light brown color.

VII. *J. Barber & Company's Mine*, Hensingerville, one and a half miles south, south-west of Alburtis. (R. P., 1874, D, p. 22.)

Limonite, compact, with large mass of fibrous ore.

VIII. *Shankweiler Lot*, at Hensingerville, 78 feet below the surface. (R. P., 1874, D, p. 23.)

Limonite, very hard and compact, slaty structure, surface somewhat velvety.

4—M.

	IX.	X.	XI.	XII.
Iron	44.600	44.500	51.250	43.000
Manganese	.576	9.280	.381	4.575
Sulphur	trace.	.019	.016	.049
Phosphorus	.151	.316	.100	.109
Insoluble residue	20.340	6.280	11.010	19.060

IX. *Thomas Iron Company's Mine*, at Hensingerville.* (R. P., 1874, D, p. 24.)

Limonite, hard, compact, and of somewhat slaty structure.

X. *Hensinger Heirs' Farm*, one and a half miles south of Alburtis. (R. P., 1874, D, p. 24.)

Limonite, bomb-shell ore, curiously honeycombed, with large amount of göthite.

XI. *Ludwig's Old Mine*, one mile west, north-west of Alburtis. (R. P., 1874, D, p. 26.)

Limonite, hard, arenaceous, with broken concretions of pipe ore.

XII. *Blank's Mine*, leased by Ludwig, Hertzog & Co., one-fourth mile north-west of Alburtis. (R. P., 1874, D, p. 27.)

Limonite, compact, arenaceous, containing cavities lined with göthite and lepidocrocite. Specimen also contained a small piece of arenaceous red hematite, and a small amount of pipe ore.

	XIII.	XIV.	XV.	XVI.
Iron	51.950	48.500	48.000	38.000
Manganese	.360	.194	.173	1.484
Sulphur	trace.	trace.	.032	.020
Phosphorus	.106	.123	.120	.108
Insoluble residue	11.430	16.560	15.950	30.970

XIII. *Reuben Romig's Mine*, leased by Allentown Iron Company, three-fourths of a mile east of New Texas. (R. P., 1874, D, p. 29.)

Limonite, compact, cellular, with considerable admixture of yellow clay.

XIV. *Werner & Reinhart's Mine*, leased by the Allentown Iron Company, one-half mile east of New Texas. (R. P., 1874, D, p. 29.)

Limonite, compact and cellular, with admixture of ochreous earth.

---

* This analysis is put down under Hensinger & Saul's Mine in Prof. Prime's report, but specimen was from Thomas Iron Company's Mine.

XV. *Werner & Reinhart's Mine*, mined by the Allentown on Company. (R. P., 1874, D, p. 29.)
Limonite, hard, arenaceous and compact.

XVI. *Milton Lauer's Mine*, leased by Carbon Iron Company. (R. P., 1874, D, p. 29.)
Limonite, hard, compact and very sandy.

	XVII.	XVIII.	XIX.	XX.
Iron	48.250	42.300	48.200	48.100
Manganese	.432	.648	.418	.360
Sulphur	.045	.026	.005	.045
Phosphorus	.025	.100	.158	.164
Insoluble residue	18.450	24.120	14.810	13.440

XVII. *Frank S. Lichtenwalner's Mine*, three-fourths of a mile ast of Alburtis. (R. P., 1874, D, p. 30.)
Limonite, compact, with nodular concretions and small seams of ochreous iron ore.

XVIII. *Elwyn Bastian's Mine*, leased by the Lehigh Iron ompany. (R. P., 1874, D, p. 31.)
Limonite, hard, compact, sandy, with considerable quartz in ne ore.

XIX. *Francis Guth's Mine*, leased by Carbon Iron Company, ree-fourths of a mile west, north-west of Wescoeville. (R. P., 874, D, p. 32.)
Limonite, hard, compact and sandy.

XX. *Francis Breinig's Mine*, one and a half miles north, orth-west of Breinigsville. (R. P., 1874, D, p. 32.)
Limonite, silicious, somewhat slaty structure, spongy-form. olor various shades of brown and brick red.

	XXI.	XXII.	XXIII.	XXIV.
Iron	57.500	58.500	45.700	48.500
Manganese	.749	.223	.648	.360
Sulphur	trace.	.084	.034	.002
Phosphorus	.165	.043	.157	.328
Insoluble residue	3.470	2.800	20.210	15.580

XXI. *Oliver Moser's Mine*, leased by Northampton Iron Company, one-third of a mile north of Breinigsville. (R. P., 1874,), p. 33.)
Limonite, compact mass of pipe ore, the pipes in some pieces eing somewhat obliterated; somewhat cellular, the cells being artially filled with yellow clay. Color dark brown generally.

XXII. *Thomas Breinig's Mine*, leased by Northampton Iron

Company, one-third mile north of Breinigsville. (R. P., 1874, D, p. 34.)

Limonite, very compact, somewhat cellular and stalactitic, botryoidal. Color various shades of brown.

XXIII. *Nathan Whitely's Mine*, one mile from Trexlertown, on road to Breinigsville. (R. P., 1874, D, p. 35.)

Limonite, hard, arenaceous; structure flaggy, some of the pieces decidedly fibrous.

XXIV. *William B. Fogel's Mine*, leased by Carbon Iron Company, one-half mile north-west of Trexlertown. (R. P., 1874, D, p. 36.)

Limonite, hard, compact, arenaceous, with somewhat laminated structure, and considerable admixture of yellow clay.

	XXV.	XXVI.	XXVII.	XXVIII.
Iron	51.750	49.300	46.600	49.000
Manganese	.309	.216	.144	.187
Sulphur	trace.	trace.	trace.	trace.
Phosphorus	.270	.235	.276	.172
Insoluble residue	10.350	15.120	19.880	15.400

XXV. *Henry Swartz and W. B. Fogel's Mine*, leased by the Crane Iron Company, at Trexlertown. (R. P., 1874, D, p. 36.)

Limonite, sandy, containing small cavities lined with göthite.

XXVI. *Alwyn Bortz's Mine*, one-half mile east of Trexlertown. (R. P., 1874, D, p. 36.)

Limonite, compact, argillaceous, with considerable admixture ochreous earth.

XXVII. *Alwyn Bortz and William Koch's Mine*, leased by Carbon Iron Company, one-half mile east of Trexlertown. (R. P., 1874, D, p. 37.)

Limonite, cellular, somewhat nodular, of a dark brown color.

XXVIII. *Jonas Grammis' Mine*, one-half mile east of Trexlertown. (R. P., 1874, D, p. 37.)

Limonite, soft and cellular, some of the cells being filled with yellow clay; partly laminated structure.

	XXIX.	XXX.	XXXI.	XXXII.
Iron	51.700	45.000	28.100	51.400
Manganese	trace.	.626	5.029	.295
Sulphur	.214	trace.	.002	.021
Phosphorus	.066	.190	.551	.233
Insoluble residue	10.550	21.900	36.430	11.290

XXIX. *Gackenbach's Mine*, leased by the Crane Iron Company, two miles north-east of Trexlertown. (R. P., 1874, D, p. 38.)

Limonite, stalactitic, cellular, sandy. Color various shades of brown and vermillion. Contains 10.83 per cent of water.

XXX. *Francis Fisher's Mine*, leased by the Coleraine Iron Company, one and a half miles north-west of Wescoeville. (R. P., 1874, D, p. 38.)

Limonite, arenaceous, exceedingly hard and tough, with nodular concretions and velvety surface.

XXXI. *J. & D. Smith's Mine*, leased by Millerstown Iron Company, one mile south, south-west of Fogelsville. (R. P., 1874, D, p. 39.)

Limonite, compact and exceedingly sandy, with considerable adhering yellow clay. Color various shades of light and dark brown.

XXXII. *Charles Miller's Mine*, three-fourth of a mile south, south-west of Fogelsville. Stripping ore. (R. P., 1874, D, p. 39.)

Limonite, arenaceous, with a large admixture of ochreous iron ore.

	XXXIII.	XXXIV.	XXXV.	XXXVI.
Iron	47.000	36.500	49.600	43.700
Manganese	7.464	2.932	.583	.763
Sulphur	.003	.031	.007	.005
Phosphorus	.630	3.135	1.288	.869
Insoluble residue	4.940	18.900	9.440	18.580

XXXIII. *J. D. Scholl & Co.'s Mine*, leased by Lehigh Valley Iron Company, one and a half miles south, south-east of Fogelsville. (R. P., 1874, D, p. 40.)

Limonite, compact, cellular, with numerous seams of ochreous earth.

XXXIV. *Jacob Steininger's Mine*, leased by James Lanigan, three-fourths of a mile south-west of Fogelsville. (R. P., 1874, D, p. 40.)

Limonite, compact, arenaceous, with considerable admixture of ferruginous clay.

XXXV. *Henry Stein's Mine*, leased by Thomas Iron Company, one mile west, south-west of Fogelsville. (R. P., 1874, D, p. 41.)

Limonite, rather compact, with considerable coating of white clay; some of the pieces of a brick red, and others of a foxy color.

XXXVI. *Jesse Laro's Mine*, leased by the Crane Iron Company, one and a half miles south-west of Fogelsville. (R. P., 1874, D, p. 41.)

Limonite, compact, arenaceous, of a very dark color.

	XXXVII.	XXXVIII.
Iron	42.800	50.400
Manganese	.252	1.203
Sulphur	.036	.002
Phosphorus	.222	.993
Insoluble residue	25.040	10.050

XXXVII. *Levi Lichtenwalner's Mine*, leased by the Crane Iron Company. (R. P., 1874, D, p. 42.)

Limonite, hard, sandy, with considerable ochreous iron ore.

XXXVIII. *Krœmlich & Lichtenwalner's Mine*, leased by the Crane Iron Company, at Fogelsville. (R. P., 1874, D, p. 42.)

Limonite, hard, cellular, the pieces being generally of a slaty structure. Color dark brown and cinnamon brown.

XXXIX.

Sesquioxide of iron	68.590=48.013 per cent iron.
Alumina	2.010
Oxide of manganese	trace.
Lime	270
Magnesia	1.480
Phosphoric acid	.340=0.149 per cent phosphorus.
Sulphuric acid	.060=0.025 per cent sulphur.
Water, combined	10.750
Water, hygroscopic	6.950
Insoluble residue	9.930
	100.380

XXXIX. *Ludwig's New Mine*, one mile from Alburtis. (R. P., 1874, D, p. 25.)

Average of six cars. Analyzed for Pennsylvania Steel Company in 1874, and published by permission of S. M. Felton, Esq., President.

Section 3.

Iron Ores of York county. Cambrian (?) and Mesozoic.

Only twelve specimens of ores have been examined from York county during the past season. Of these seven were limonite ore, showing an average of 44.88 per cent of iron. They are generally very rich in phosphorus, and where used alone will be apt to produce a very cold-short iron. The mean average per cent of phosphorus is 0.857. The two magnetic ores examined are of excellent quality and admirably adapted for the manufacture of Bessemer pig iron, owing to their freedom from phosphorus. By roasting the greater part of the sulphur will be eliminated.

	I.	II.	III.
Sesquioxide of iron	64.428	61.428	72.143
Sesquioxide of manganese	2.150	5.570	.387
Alumina	3.148	3.176	1.725
Lime	.140	.157	.168
Magnesia	.270	.155	.330
Sulphuric acid	.230	.256	.123
Phosphoric acid	1.374	1.546	.432
Water	11.020	11.010	5.760
Insoluble residue	16.950	16.600	19.090
	99.710	99.878	100.158
Iron	45.100	43.000	50.500
Manganese	1.490	4.004	.269
Sulphur	.090	.054	.049
Phosphorus	.610	.675	.189

I. *Bollinger Bank*, four miles north-east of Hanover. (R. P. 1874, C, p. 56.)

Limonite, sandy, shelly, with cavities filled with göthite and lepidocrocite.

II. *Haldeman Bank*, five miles north-east of Hanover, at the foot of Pigeon Hill. (R. P., 1874, C, p. 60.)

Limonite, sandy, full of seams of ochreous iron, and with small masses of göthite and lepidocrocite.

III. *Haldeman Bank*, (red oxide,) five miles north-east of Hanover, at foot of Pigeon Hill. (R. P., 1874, C, p. 62.)

Red hematite, arenaceous, exceedingly hard and tough.

	IV.	V.	VI.
Sesquioxide of iron	63.285	69.714	67.000
Sesquioxide of manganese	2.210	1.135	2.341
Alumina	.765	1.422	.950
Lime	.196	.106	1.680
Magnesia	.216	.194	.591
Sulphuric acid	.068	.095	.277
Phosphoric acid	2.986	.844	2.804
Water	10.880	11.100	11.890
Insoluble residue	19.750	15.630	12.320
	100.356	100.240	99.853
Iron	44.300	48.800	46.900
Manganese	1.538	.790	1.630
Sulphur	.024	.038	.110
Phosphorus	1.303	.343	1.224

IV. *Fritz Bank*, three and three quarter miles north-east of York. (R. P., 1874, C, p. 50.)

Limonite, compact, with cavities filled with ochreous iron ore and ferruginous clay.

V. *Magaretta Bank*, near Margaretta furnace, five and a half miles south-east of Wrightsville. (R. P., 1874, C, p. 21.)

Limonite, brittle, arenaceous, with more or less decomposed argillaceous slaty gangue.

VI. *Early & Killinger Mine*, two and a half miles east of Littlestown. (R. P., 1874, C, p. 44.)

Limonite, with cavities containing nodular lumps, the sides of the walls consisting of göthite and lepidocrocite; shell-like structure, and containing a considerable admixture of quartz.

	VII.	VIII.
Sesquioxide of iron	46.285	76.714
Sesquioxide of manganese	21.888	.640
Alumina	2.674	......
Lime	.240	......
Magnesia	.155	......
Baryta	1.322	......
Sulphuric acid	......	trace.
Phosphoric acid	1.491	2.741
Water	11.200	......
Insoluble residue	14.780	3.710
	100.035	......
Iron	32.400	53.700
Manganese	15.239	.446
Sulphur	......	trace.
Phosphorus	.651	1.197

ANALYSES OF IRON ORES.

VII. *Smyser Bank*, four miles north, north-east of York. (R. P., 1874, C, p. 67.)

Limonite, fine grained, with conchoidal fracture, and containing masses of göthite.

VIII. *M'Nair's Ore*, about eight miles south of Gettysburg, on Emmitsburg road. (R. P., 1874, C, p. 76.)

Limonite, hard, compact, fine grained. Color dark brown. Surface somewhat velvety.

IX.

Protoxide of iron	10.475
Sesquioxide of iron	7.324
Bisulphide of iron	1.818
Bisulphide of copper	.060
Protoxide of manganese	.480
Alumina	7.391
Lime	6.350
Magnesia	5.686
Alkalies	2.190
Carbonic acid	4.420
Sulphuric acid	.016
Phosphoric acid	.201
Titanic acid	1.260
Water	2.142
Silica	50.150
	99.963
Iron	14.125
Sulphur	.988
Phosphorus	.088

Magnetite separated by magnet, 4.36 per cent.

IX. *Help Bank*, (so-called "Nes Silicon Steel Ore") two-thirds of a mile north of Shrewsbury, on Northern Central railroad. (R. P., 1874, C, p. 10.)

Calcareous chloritic rock, compact, of a greenish color, containing crystals of magnetite, pyrite and calcite.

X.

Protoxide of iron	.900	} 36.300 per cent iron.
Sesquioxide of iron	50.857	
Sesquioxide of manganese	.103	
Alumina	1.630	
Lime	.862	
Magnesia	.303	
Sulphuric acid	.011=	.004 per cent sulphur.
Phosphoric acid	.513=	.224 per cent phosphorus.
Water	1.690	
Insoluble residue	43.425	
	100.294	

Insoluble residue:	X.	
Silica	36.990	
Alumnia	4.090	
Oxide of iron	1.310=	.917 per cent iron.
Lime	.050	
Magnesia	.510	

X. *York Iron Co.'s Mine*, near Strickhouser station, on Hanover Junction railroad, (so called " Codorus Ore.") (R. P., 1874, C, p. 32.)

Micaceous hematite, or rather hydro-mica slate bearing considerable oxide of iron; shows a few crystals of magnetite, also spangles of specular oxide of iron; rather friable, slaty structure, the slate being very much decomposed.

	XI.	XII.
Protoxide of iron	18.643	18.385
Sesquioxide of iron	42.100	43.414
Bisulphide of iron	4.093	.450
Sulphide of copper	.098 Oxide of copper.	trace.
Sulphide of cobalt	.766 Oxide of cobalt.	.326
Alumina	2.417	2.774
Protoxide of manganese	.186	.352
Lime	6.132	7.563
Magnesia	6.738	5.001
Potash and soda	.350	.054
Carbonic acid	1.760	1.640
Sulphuric acid	.119	.011
Phosphoric acid	.052	.052
Water	1.080	2.320
Silica	15.120	17.860
	99.654	100.202
Iron	45.880	44.900
Sulphur	2.680	.244
Phosphorus	.023	.023

XI. *Logan's Shaft*, one mile north-east of Dillsburg. "Mumper ore." (R. P., 1874, C, p. 71.)

Magnetite, compact, of a sea-green color, carrying a large amount of pyrite and considerable calcite. Sample in part strongly crystalline magnetite and part as magnetic sand.

XII. *Fuller's Mine*, on bank of Yellow Breeches creek, three miles north-east of Dillsburg. (R. P., 1874, C, p. 74.)

Magnetite, hard and compact, carrying considerable calcite. Specimen contains considerable magnetic sand.

Analyses of Ignited "Insoluble Residue" in Iron Ores.

	Silica	Alumina	Oxide of iron	Lime	Magnesia	Sulphate of Baryta,	Per cent insoluble residue
Bollinger Bank, four miles north-east of Hanover	14.37	1.59	.21	.02	.24		16.95
Haldeman Bank, five miles north-east of Hanover	14.24	1.57	.31	.01	.14		16.60
Haldeman Bank, "Red oxide,"	16.16	1.78	.72	.05	.25		19.09
Fritz Bank, three and three quarter miles north-east of York	15.25	3.23	.17	.04	.63		19.75
Margaretta Bank, five and a half miles south-east of Wrightsville	12.87	1.83	.25	.02	.50		15.63
Early & Killinger Mine, two and a half miles east of Littlestown	11.17	.61	.01	.07	.12		12.32
Smyser Bank, four miles north, north-east of York	11.19	2.23	.30	.02	.39	.202	14.78

	XIII.	XIV.
Ferrous oxide	13.930	20.130
Ferric oxide	45.640	44.732
Iron di-sulphide	1.052	.742
Alumina	1.824	1.050
Manganous oxide	.652	trace.
Lime	5.322	1.484
Magnesia	4.308	1.837
Oxide of copper	.048	trace.
Phosphoric acid	.024	.038
Water	5.000	1.580
Silica	22.100	27.700
	99.900	99.293
Metallic iron	42.750	47.314
Sulphur	.590	.361
Phosphorus	.011	.018

XIII. "*Dillsburg Ore*," Alex. Underwood's mine, at Dillsburg. (R. P., 1874, C, p. 73.)

Analyzed for the Penn'a Steel Co. in 1873, and published by permission of S. M. Felton, Esq., president.

XIV. "*Dillsburg Ore*," Alex. Underwood's mine, at Dillsburg. (R. P., 1874, C, p. 73.)

Analyzed for Penn'a Steel Co., in 1872, and published by permission.

Section 4.

Fossil Ores of the Juniata. Silurian.

Eighteen samples of fossil ore have been examined from Mifflin and Huntingdon counties. Many of these ores are of excellent quality, containing over 50 per cent iron and with little injurious admixtures present. Others again contain such a large amount of carbonate of lime as to be only ferriferous limestones. The average per cent of iron in the eighteen samples is 35.59. The percentage of phosphorus is usually quite low, the mean average being .277 per cent.

When no carbonate of lime is noted in the analysis, its absence in the ore may always be understood.

The amount of manganese present in these ores is usually very small, a number of tests made showing a mere trace.

Mifflin County.

	I.	II.	III.	IV.
Iron	16.000	36.400	44.400	34.000
Sulphur	.024	.017	.028	.018
Phosphorus	.230	.184	.115	.124
Insoluble residue	58.370	35.200	28.880	35.480

I. *George M'Kee's Ore Bank*, Ferguson valley, seven miles west of Yeagertown; lower portion of fossil ore vein 16 inches thick.

Compact, highly silicious fossil ore of a light brown color.

II. *George M'Kee's Ore Bank*, Ferguson valley, seven miles west of Yeagertown; top portion of ore vein good; whole vein about 18 inches thick; this part analyzed about 10 inches thick.

Compact, silicious fossil ore of a dark brown color.

III. *George M'Kee's Ore Bank*, Ferguson valley, seven miles west of Yeagertown; fossil ore vein 12 inches thick; this part (top) eight inches thick; north dip in vein. Balance, four inches in "Jack."

Compact, sandy fossil ore of a reddish brown color.

IV. *North of George M'Kee's Ore Bank*, near Jas. Shehan's house, in the meadow foot of Jack's mountain. Ore vein about 12 inches thick; second specimen taken from heap of ore, being ore from shaft. Specimens mixed in proper proportions previous to analysis.

Compact, sandy, fossil ore of a deep red color.

	V.
Sesquioxide of iron	42.857
Alumina	7.816
Sesquioxide of manganese	.093
Lime	.448
Magnesia	.738
Phosphoric acid	.547
Sulphuric acid	.122
Water	5.500
Insoluble residue	41.510
	99.631
Iron	30.000
Sulphur	.048
Phosphorus	.239

V. *George M'Kee's Ore Bank*, Ferguson Valley, seven miles west of Yeagertown. Top bench of vein six to twelve inches thick; bottom part of vein, lower bench, two to six inches thick; face of gangway eight to twelve inches thick; top bench, south dip, average of vein. The analysis represents the above ores mixed in proper proportions. Compact, coarse, sandy fossil ore of a deep red color; somewhat slaty.

	VI.	VII.	VIII.	IX.
Iron	39.800	42.300	59.100	27.500
Sulphur	.011	.010	trace.	trace.
Phosphorus	.231	.516	.110	.206
Insoluble residue	31.560	25.930	7.470	43.110

VI. *John Kinzer's Ore Bank*, five miles north-east from M'Veytown. Soft fossil ore (medium;) north dip; south anticlinal of ore ridge; vein one foot thick.

Fossil ore, compact, iron rust color, with a tendency to break up into blocks.

VII. *Ferguson Valley Ore Ridge*, six miles north-east from M'Veytown. Fossil ore, (medium soft;) John M'Cord ore bank, No. 2 gangway.

Fossil ore, compact and very hard, reddish brown color, slaty structure with much slaty gangue.

VIII. *Ferguson Valley*, six miles north-east from M'Veytown. Iron ore found within the ore sandstone, six inches thick at M'Cord ore bank.

Fossil ore, compact, very earthy appearance, exceedingly tough, and of a brown color.

IX. *Ferguson Valley*, six miles north-east of M'Veytown ore ridge. John M'Cord ore bank, north dip; faulty vein.

Fossil ore, very argillaceous, structure somewhat slaty with delicate pink color.

	X.	XI.	XII.
Iron	13.100	23.000	40.900
Sulphur	.018	.054	.014
Phosphorus	.252	.268	1.018
Carbonate of lime	54.792	31.272	18.136
Carbonate of magnesia	1.428	4.080	1.408
Insoluble residue	15.992	25.392	12.976

X. *Matilda Furnace*, one mile north from Mt. Union. Fossiliferous ore from No. 3; under ore sandstone, 10 inches thick.

Fossil ore, hard and compact, with adhering slate; part of specimen is iron rust color, and part of a light gray.

Analyzed by S. A. Ford.

XI. *Matilda Furnace*, one mile north of Mt. Union. Hard fossil ore taken from the water level gangway, 16 inches thick at the opening; size irregular.

Fossil ore, very hard and compact, chocolate color, containing particles of slate.

Analyzed by S. A. Ford.

XII. *Matilda Furnace*, one mile north of Mt. Union. Hard fossil ore taken from lower level gangway.

Fossil ore, hard and compact, of a slaty structure and red color.

Analyzed by S. A. Ford.

	XIII.	XIV.
Iron	41.700	50.000
Sulphur	.034	.024
Phosphorus	.212	.606
Insoluble residue	27.640	14.784

XIII. *Ferguson Valley*, six miles north-east of M'Veytown. John Rothrick ore bank, (soft medium fossil.) In same ravine as John M'Cord ore bank, on east side of ravine; north dip of ore ridge; vein from 16 to 18 inches thick.

Fossil ore, hard and compact, slaty structure, reddish brown color, containing numerous particles of specular iron ore.

Analyzed by S. A. Ford.

ANALYSES OF FOSSIL ORES. M. 63

XIV. *Matilda Furnace*, one mile north from Mt. Union. Medium fossil taken from third level; vein 20 to 22 inches thick; vein overlying the ore s. s.

Fossil ore, compact, with slaty gangue; color brownish red; ore has a tendency to break up into blocks.

Analyzed by S. A. Ford.

Huntingdon County.

	XV.	XVI.
Sesquioxide of iron	72.571	72.428
Alumina	4.723	4.211
Sesquioxide of manganese	.320	.269
Lime	.174	.319
Magnesia	.309	.432
Phosphoric acid	.256	.281
Sulphuric acid	trace.	trace.
Water	3.440	4.620
Insoluble residue	18.650	17.000
	100.443	99.560
Iron	50.800	50.700
Sulphur	trace.	trace.
Phosphorus	.112	.123

XV. *South side of Blacklog Gap*, No. 1 gangway, large underlying fossil ore; vein 20 inches in thickness. Rockhill Coal and Iron Company.

Compact, coarse fossil ore, reddish brown color.

XVI. *South side of Blacklog Gap*, small overlying fossil ore vein; gangway No. 1. Rockhill Coal and Iron Company.

Hard, compact fossil ore, chocolate brown color, with somewhat laminated structure.

	XVII.	XVIII.
Iron	23.800	27.250
Sulphur	trace.	trace.
Phosphorus	.238	.203
Carbonate of lime	39.132	36.007
Carbonate of magnesia	6.976	1.180
Insoluble residue	12.850	16.610

XVII. *Blacklog Gap*, near Orbisonia. No. 1 north gangway. Hard fossil ore.

Fossil ore, hard, compact, reddish color.

XVIII. *North side of Blacklog Gap*, near Orbisonia. Bottom vein, drift No. 1, 20 inches thick.

Fossil ore, hard, compact, with numerous small crystals of calcite; of a reddish brown color.

Section 5.

Brown Hematite Ores of the Juniata. Devonian.

Twenty-three brown hematite ores have been examined from these counties. The percentage of iron found varies from 20.62, present in a *bog ore*, to 51.90 per cent, found in the ore from Dull & Bradley's Mine. The mean average per cent of the twenty-three specimens is 39.13.

The ores are generally silicious, having 27.28 as the mean average per cent of insoluble residue.

The amount of phosphorus is in most cases quite small, the average per cent being (exclusive of the bog ore) 0.284.

Mifflin County.

	I.	II.	III.	IV.
Iron	25.000	42.500	30.900	29.500
Sulphur	.257	.044	.035	.062
Phosphorus	.688	.078	.107	.039
Insoluble residue	47.230	23.890	44.140	44.380

I. *Lewistown Section*, on wagon road north-west of Lewistown. Ore shaft.

Compact, argillaceous limonite of a light brown color.

II. *M'Veytown Gap*, Ross ore opening. Ore from upper opening.

Limonite, compact, argillaceous, of a light brown color.

III. *James Rhodes*, in Kansas property, on hill south of his house. Ore opening in Oriskany hil¹

Limonite, compact, arenaceous, of a deep brown color.

IV. *James Rhodes' Ore Opening*, Kansas, opposite his house. Second vein cut in tunnel. Vein from one to five feet.

Limonite, very sandy, slaty structure, and somewhat friable.

	V.	VI.	VII.	VIII.	IX.
Iron	46.500	51.900	44.700	50.000	26.000
Sulphur	.028	.033	.008	.058	.046
Phosphorus	.349	.231	.165	.166	.588
Insoluble residue	13.830	8.970	19.950	11.456	47.232

V. *Kansas ore*, north of James Rhodes' house, picked from surface, being an ore common on surface of Jack's mountain.

Limonite, hard and sandy. Surface ore.

VI. *Dull & Bradley Mine*, one mile east of Dunkard church. Lime ridge, south of Ferguson valley; ore from shaft. Vein three to five feet thick.

Limonite, compact, containing a small admixture of ochreous iron ore; one of the pieces being section of a geode.

VII. "*Squaw Hollow*," three and half miles north-west from Lewistown. Moore's ore bank. Vein two to three feet thick. Mined by Logan Iron Company.

Limonite, compact, with much adhering clay; structure somewhat laminated, part of the specimen being beautifully stalactitic.

VIII. *On Williams' Farm*, four and a half miles east from Logan steel works; north synclinal.

Limonite, compact, surface covered with ochreous earth, somewhat stalactitic. Color dark brown.

Analyzed by S. A. Ford.

IX. *Barnhart Bank*, four miles west of Lewistown. Silicious hematite overlying the Oriskany sandstone, two to four feet thick.

Limonite, silicious, with much adhering clay; structure laminated. Color chocolate brown.

Analyzed by S. A. Ford.

	X.
Sesquioxide of iron	62.143
Alumina	3.795
Sesquioxide of manganese	.651
Lime	.722
Magnesia	.360
Phosphoric acid	1.362
Sulphuric acid	.053
Water	11.390
Insoluble residue	19.690
	100.166
Iron	43.500
Sulphur	.021
Phosphorus	.595

X. First synclinal on Lewistown section, one mile north-west of Lewistown. Marcellus vein.

Limonite, containing cavities filled with ferruginous clay.

66 M.   A. S. M'CREATH.   REPORT OF 1874-'75.

	XI.
Sesquioxide of iron	29.464
Alumina	5.639
Oxide of manganese	14.902
Lime	.280
Magnesia	.335
Baryta	.204
Phosphoric acid	3.037
Water	23.270
Insoluble residue	22.840
	99.971
Iron	20.625
Manganese	10.375
Sulphur	.034
Phosphorus	1.326

XI. *Bog ore,* Kansas, along side, and east and west of James Rhodes' house, five miles north-west of M'Veytown; ore one to three feet thick.

Bog ore, compact, sandy, of a deep brown color. This ore was tested for organic acids, but no appreciable quantity was found.

Huntingdon County.

	XII.	XIII.	XIV.	XV.
Iron	42.200	33.250	39.000	47.500
Sulphur	.122	trace.	.095	trace.
Phosphorus	.130	.345	.096	.402
Carbonate of lime	.990			
Carbonate of magnesia	.756			
Insoluble residue	19.740	41.750	28.210	17.260

XII. *Ore from Orbison Slope,* Sandy Ridge, near Orbisonia. Limonite, hard, cellular, with much adhering clay.

XIII. *Chert Ore Bank,* east of Broad Top railroad, Sandy Ridge, two miles south from Orbisonia. Ore from Oriskany shales. Rockhill Coal and Iron Company

Limonite, hard, compact and silicious.

XIV. *Mountain Boulder Ore,* on terrace of Blacklog mountain, near Orbisonia, north-east of Blacklog Gap. Rockhill Coal and Iron Company.

Limonite, compact, silicious, surface somewhat velvety.

XV. *Lane Ore Bank,* Hill Valley, five miles north-west from Orbisonia. Ore in Oriskany sandstone, lower portion Chestnut Ridge. Lane property.

Limonite, sandy, with large admixture of ochreous earth.

ANALYSES OF HEMATITE ORES.

	XVI.	XVII.	XVIII.	XIX.
Iron	47.500	47.300	45.000	51.700
Sulphur	.013	trace.	.032	.023
Phosphorus	.111	.491	.187	.068
Insoluble residue	14.100	17.900	26.580	10.490

XVI. *Hick's Ore Bank*, between Logan ore bank and Stewart's ore, five miles from Orbisonia, Chestnut ridge. Rockhill Coal and Iron Company.

Limonite, cellular, cells for the most part filled with ochreous ore.

XVII. *Douglas Ore Bank*, opposite Lane ore bank, five miles north-west from Orbisonia.

Limonite, compact, silicious and cellular.

XVIII. *Mountain Ore Bank*, four miles south-west from Orbisonia, in crevice of Medina sandstone, Blacklog mountain. Rockhill Coal and Iron Company.

Limonite, compact, botryoidal, somewhat cellular; color various shades of brown.

XIX. *Sandy Ridge Ore*, two miles north from Orbisonia. Rockhill Coal and Iron Company.

Limonite, very hard and compact, containing considerable ochreous iron ore; dark brown color.

	XX.	XXI.	XXII.	XXIII.
Iron	34.800	37.900	33.300	29.800
Sulphur	trace.	.010	.126	.060
Phosphorus	.726	.386	.238	.082
Manganese	3.006	.915	......	......
Insoluble residue	25.010	31.300	43.752	48.190

XX. *Martin Ore Bank*, Hill valley, south-west from Logan farm, five miles from Orbisonia, on terrace of Jack's mountain. Iron ore in lower Clinton shales on Martin ore land.

Limonite, silicious, rather compact, with light brown color.

XXI. *Whitzel's Ore Opening*, on terrace of Jack's mountain, north of "Logan Farm" ore bank, five miles from Orbisonia. Ore in Clinton shales.

Limonite, exceedingly silicious, with laminated structure.

XXII. *Mt. Union*, Jack's Narrows, one mile north from Mt. Union. "Bog" from loose rocks from red Medina sandstone.

Limonite, very hard, cellular, containing masses of quartz; iridescent, with dark brown color.

Analyzed by S. A. Ford.

XXIII. *Wilson Farm*, Hill valley, five miles north-west from Orbisonia. Iron ore from the seam of Oriskany sandstone.

Limonite, silicious, exceedingly hard and tough; structure somewhat laminated; color reddish brown.

Section 6.

Brown Hematite Ores of the Coal Measures.

Only five specimens of brown hematite ores have been examined from the coal measures. They are generally of good quality, yielding as the mean average 39.74 per cent of iron.

In only two cases is there an appreciable amount of manganese present. The per cent of phosphorus is generally large, showing 0.444 as the mean average of the five samples examined.

Only one specimen of *red hematite* has been examined from the coal measures. It yielded 57 per cent metallic iron, but is not supposed to exist in any great quantity. It is interesting, however, to notice this in connection with Dr. T. Sterry Hunt's discovery of several specimens of this valuable ore in the coal measures of the Hocking valley, Ohio.

Clearfield County.

	I.	II.
Iron	42.400	40.800
Sulphur	.039	trace.
Phosphorus	.082	.596
Insoluble residue	23.120	25.600

I. *Lambert's Ore*, on Clearfield creek, seven miles above mouth. (R. P., 1874, H, p. 100.)

Limonite ore, of a reddish brown color, compact, laminated structure.

II. *Leightner's Ore*, on Clearfield creek, five miles south-west of Glen Hope. From outcrop near hill top. (R. P., 1874, H, p. 108.)

Limonite ore, hard, compact, silicious and of a dark brown color.

Jefferson County.

	III.	IV.
Iron	36.800	37.700
Manganese	1.744	2.212
Sulphur	.034	018
Phosphorus	.296	.553
Insoluble residue	22.980	20.770

III. *Bovaird's Ore,* three and a half miles west of Brockway ville, on top of limestone bed. (R. P., 1874, H, p. 222.)

Limonite, compact, highly fossiliferous, of a reddish brown color.

IV. *Bovaird's Ore,* fossils in ore on top of limestone. (R. P., 1874, H, p. 223.)

Limonite, compact, highly fossiliferous, of a reddish brown color; almost the entire mass being made up of closely packed fossil forms.

Centre County.

	V.
Iron	41.000
Sulphur	trace.
Phosphorus	.692
Insoluble residue	25.250

V. *Brown hematite ore* just west of the summit of the Allegheny mountain, on line of Bellefonte and Snow Shoe railroad. (R. P., 1874, H, p. 78.)

Limonite ore, brittle, arenaceous, of a light brown color.

Section 7.

Carbonate Ores of the Juniata. Devonian.

Five specimens of carbonate ores from Mifflin and Huntingdon counties have been examined during the past season. The general excellence of their character is at once apparent on glancing at the analyses given in the following tables.

The mean average per cent of iron is 36.78.

The amount of phosphorus present is unusually small, the average percentage being 0.189. When thoroughly roasted these ores will yield from 45 to 60 per cent metallic iron. One of the specimens from the Ross ore bank shows an ore of unusual purity; when thoroughly roasted it yields 60 per cent metallic iron. The small amount of injurious ingredients present will allow the profitable production of an excellent quality of metal. It is curious to notice how this ore is oxidized, and its character entirely changed in some parts of the bed. An analysis of the limonite ore found associated with it gives 42.50 per cent of iron and 0.078 per cent of phosphorus.

Mifflin County.

	I.	II.
Iron	33.500	42.500
Sulphur	.734	.260
Phosphorus	.110	.135
Insoluble residue	18.870	3.390

I. *Ross Ore Bank*, M'Veytown gap, one mile north of M'Veytown. Black carbonate ore; lower depths of vein. Here this specimen alternates with shale and, including the yellow hematite, measures from 24 to 28 feet.

Carbonate ore, exceedingly hard and compact, surface somewhat hematitic and botryoidal, structure laminated, and fracture conchoidal; color various shades of black. The ore carries considerable carbonaceous matter.

II. *Ross Ore Bank*, M'Veytown gap, one mile north from M'Veytown. Carbonate ore, upper portion in layers divided by black shale. Whole thickness of measures, including alternations, 24 to 28 feet

Carbonate ore, hard and compact, color bluish-black, crust hematitic, fracture conchoidal, showing small crystals of pyrites. Ore carries considerable carbonaceous matter, and when thoroughly roasted yields sixty per cent metallic iron, and five per cent insoluble silicious residue.

	III.
Protoxide of iron	48.857
Sesquioxide of iron	.825
Bisulphide of iron	.262
Alumina	2.240
Protoxide of manganese	1.625
Lime	4.536
Magnesia	.569
Phosphoric acid	1.314
Sulphuric acid	.133
Carbonic acid	32.650
Water	.368
Organic matter	.360
Insoluble residue	6.410
	100.149
Iron	38.700
Sulphur	.192
Phosphorus	.574

III. *Lewistown Section*, one mile north-west of Lewistown. Carbonate ore taken from near the surface.

Clay iron ore, steel gray color, hard and compact, with conchoidal fracture.

Huntingdon County.

	IV.	V.
Iron	35.500	33.700
Sulphur	.480	.533
Phosphorus	.081	.045
Insoluble residue	14.790	18.520

IV. *Near Hill Valley*, five miles west from Orbisonia, Chestnut Ridge. "Logan farm" bank. Marcellus ore vein.

Clay iron ore, carbonate, compact, cellular, and of a light gray color.

V. *Orbison Slope*, Sandy Ridge, near Orbisonia. Rockhill Coal and Iron Co.

Carbonate ore, compact, somewhat slaty structure, with small seams of limonite.

Section 8.

Carbonate Ores of the Coal Measures.

Thirteen carbonate ores from the coal measures have been examined during the past season. They are rather lean, but when roasted will yield sufficient iron to be profitably worked in the blast furnace. From their convenience to the fuel and flux necessary for their smelting, the day cannot be far distant when these ores must play a prominent part in the iron industries of the United States.

By being roasted they lose their carbonic acid and other volatile ingredients, and as the fragments of ore retain very nearly their original size and form, they thereby acquire a degree of porosity which materially facilitates their after reduction in the blast furnace. They usually contain quite an appreciable amount of foreign admixtures, such as lime and magnesia, which are in themselves valuable adjuncts in the blast furnace. The mean average per cent of iron of the thirteen specimens examined is 30.30.

The amount of sulphur and phosphorus generally present is in most cases quite small, so that the product from their smelting ought to be a foundry iron of excellent quality.

Only one sample of so called *blackband* ore has been examined during the past season. A partial analysis of it is given in No. III, of these tables. A complete analysis of this ore has been made by Mr. Frederick W. Forman, under my direction, and the results are here given as showing the true character of the ore. For comparison, an analysis of the blackband ore from Low Moor, Yorkshire, analyzed by Mr. J. Spiller, is also given. It is interesting to notice how closely the two analyses correspond. The amount of carbonaceous matter present is small compared with the famous Scotch blackband ironstone. In order to make the comparison complete, an analysis of this latter made by me in 1868, in the Laboratory of the late Professor Penny, Glasgow, is added to the tables.

Centre County.

	I.	II.	III.	IV.
Iron	30.250	35.800	29.300	28.700
Sulphur	.112	trace.	.010	.011
Phosphorus	.211	.204	.201	.178
Insoluble residue	19.630	16.050	17.600	23.600

I. *Yeager's Ore*, one and a half miles west of Snow Shoe City. (R. P., 1874, H, p. 76.)

Carbonate ore, compact, minutely crystalline, dark gray color, with conchoidal fracture.

II. *M'Master's Ore*, near Snow Shoe City. (R. P., 1874, H, p. 76.)

Carbonate ore, hard, minutely crystalline, of a steel gray color and conchoidal fracture.

III. *Snow Shoe Basin*, ore overlying Bed C, Mine No. 1. (R. P., 1874, H, p. 77.)

Carbonate ore. Color various shades of brown and black. Structure slaty, very hard and compact. A specimen of this ore when thoroughly roasted in the Laboratory, yielded 43 per cent metallic iron.

IV. *Snow Shoe Basin*, Clayband ore, underlying middle bed of coal. (R. P., 1874, H, p. 77.)

Carbonate ore, hard and compact, of a dark color and slaty structure.

	V.	VI.
Iron	30.100	32.600
Sulphur	.086	.013
Phosphorus	.364	.993
Insoluble residue	23.250	20.530

V. *Snow Shoe Basin*. Ore underlying Mine No. 4. Ore overlying Coal Bed A. (R. P., 1874, H. p. 77.)

Carbonate ore, hard and compact, minutely crystalline, steel gray color, with conchoidal fracture.

VI. *Snow Shoe Basin.* Ore underlying Mine No. 4. (R. P. 1874, H, p. 77.)

Carbonate ore, hard and compact, steel gray color and conchoidal fracture.

Clearfield County.

	VII.	VIII.
Iron	34.000	34.000
Sulphur	.054	.061
Phosphorus	.221	.356
Insoluble residue	21.040	18.050

VII. *Karthaus Mine*, near Karthaus P. O. (R. P., 1874, H, p. 82.)

Red ore, abandoned drift, from loose ore lying in front.

Carbonate ore, surface hematitic, hard and compact, nodular, concentric.

VIII. *J. Leightner's Ore*, on Clearfield creek, five miles south west of Glen Hope. (R. P., 1874, H, p. 107.)

Ore from lower bed 60 feet above creek.

Carbonate ore, minutely crystalline, of a dark steel gray color and conchoidal fracture.

Jefferson County.

	IX.	X	XI.
Iron	34.000	21.100	27.000
Sulphur	.355	.127	.053
Phosphorus	.202	.433	.108
Insoluble residue	11.390	30.010	31.120

IX. *Hog Shanty Run Ore*, seven miles west, south-west of Reynoldsville. (R. P., 1874, H, p. 168.)

Carbonate ore, exceedingly hard and compact, minutely crystalline, of a dark gray color, with conchoidal fracture, and showing crystals of iron pyrites.

X. *Clayville Iron Ore*, in bed of Mahoning creek, three-fourths of a mile west of Punxatawney. Ore resting on limestone. (R. P., 1874, H, p. 183.)

Carbonate ore, compact, silicious, of a greenish gray color, and showing crystals of pyrites.

XI. *P. Galusha Ore*, on Toby creek, three miles north-west of Brockwayville. (R. P., 1874, H, p. 221.)

Carbonate ore, hard, compact and silicious, light gray in color, and with conchoidal fracture.

Indiana County.

	XII.
Iron	26.500
Sulphur	.141
Phosphorus	.149
Insoluble residue	34.460

XII. *Schlimmer's Iron Ore*, Canoe township, three and a half miles south-east of Punxatawney. (R. P., 1874, H, p. 185.) Carbonate ore, hard, compact and silicious, of a bluish gray color and conchoidal fracture.

Clarion County.

	XIII.
Iron	30.600
Sulphur	.075
Phosphorus	.225
Insoluble residue	18.300

XIII. *Himes' Ore*, New Bethlehem, Red Bank creek, Low Grade railroad. (R. P., 1874, H, p. 234.) Carbonate ore, hard, compact, and of a dark gray color and conchoidal fracture.

Blackband Iron Ores.

	I.	II.	III.
Ferric oxide	4.127	1.450	0.750
Ferrous oxide	33.171	36.140	35.390
Manganous oxide	1.962	1.380	1.860
Alumina	3.347	6.740	.410
Lime	3.494	2.700	2.010
Magnesia	2.021	2.170	.860
Potash	......	.650	......
Silica	20.160	17.370	6.400
Carbonic acid	25.950	26.570	24.950
Phosphoric acid	.513	.340	.510
Sulphuric acid	trace.	trace.	......
Iron pyrites	.024	.100	trace.
Water { hygroscopic.. { combined....	1.650	{ .610 { 1.160	.400
Carbonaceous matter	2.730	2.400	26.800
	99.149	99.780	100.340
Metallic iron	28.700	29.100	27.520

I. *Snow Shoe Basin*, Centre county. Blackband ore overlying bed C. Analyzed by Fred'k W. Forman.

II. *Blackband from Low Moor*, in Yorkshire. Analyzed by J. Spiller.

III. *Scotch blackband ironstone*. Analyzed by A. S. M'Creath.

CHAPTER III.

LIMESTONES.

Method of Analysis.

1. *Insoluble Residue.*—One gramme of the finely pulverized limestone is dissolved in hydrochloric acid and the solution evaporated to dryness; re-dissolved in dilute acid, and the insoluble residue filtered off. This is washed thoroughly, dried, ignited and weighed.

2. *Iron and Alumina.*—The iron and alumina in the filtrate are precipitated with a slight excess of ammonia, the solution boiled, and the precipitate filtered off. This is dissolved in a small quantity of acid, and re-precipitated with ammonia. The filtrate from this is added to the other. The precipitate of iron and alumnia is thoroughly washed, ignited and weighed. A separation is best made, when the iron is in small quantities, by the method given in the analysis of fire-clay. The second precipitation of the iron and alumina is made, as a small quantity of lime is invariably carried down by the first precipitation.

3. *Lime.*—The two filtrates from the iron and alumina are treated with an excess of oxalate of ammonia, and the precipitate after being allowed to stand aside for some time, is filtered off and washed thoroughly. It is then burned off, the resulting carbonate of lime dissolved in a small quantity of hydrochloric acid, and the lime precipitated from the solution by an excess of sulphuric acid and alcohol The mixture is allowed to stand aside for twelve hours, after which the sulphate of lime is filtered off, washed with alcohol and water, dried, ignited and weighed. From the weight of the sulphate of lime found the amount of lime is calculated.

4. *Magnesia.*—The magnesia is estimated in the filtrate from the oxalate of lime precipitate, by being thrown down in a strongly ammoniacal solution by means of phosphate of soda. The solution is allowed to stand aside for twelve hours, after which the precipitate is filtered off, washed with ammonia

water, dried, ignited and weighed. From the weight of the phosphate obtained the per cent of magnesia is calculated.

5. *Sulphur and Phosphorus* are estimated by the methods as given under iron ores.

Lehigh county.

	I.	II.	III.	IV.
Carbonate of lime	51.920	47.890	51.603	48.630
Carbonate of magnesia	41.071	39.585	32.917	40.410
Sulphur	trace.	trace.	.147	.005
Phosphorus	.011	.021	.012	.012
Insoluble residue	5.650	11.260	13.490	9.240

I. *Thomas Iron Co.'s Quarry*, three-fourths of a mile north, north-west of Alburtis. (R. P., 1874, D, p. 12.)

Limestone, hard, compact, and of a bluish gray color.

II. *Thomas Iron Co.'s Quarry*, three-fourths of a mile north-east of Alburtis. (R. P., 1874, D, p. 12.)

Limestone, compact, highly crystalline, and of a bluish gray color.

III. *Mrs. Kuhn's Quarry*, one and a half miles north-east of Trexlertown. (R. P., 1874, D, p. 12.)

Limestone, compact, silicious, and of a light bluish gray color.

IV. *Frantz Quarry*, one and a half miles north-east of Trexlertown. (R. P., 1874, D, p. 12.)

Limestone, hard, silicious, of a dark blue color.

Centre County.

	V.	VI.
Carbonate of lime	42.941	51.153
Carbonate of magnesia	22.764	13.265
Sulphur	.599	trace.
Phosphorus	.050	.287
Insoluble residue	18.730	23.530

V. *Snow Shoe Basin*, Freeport limestone underlying ore. (R. P., 1874, H, p. 76.)

Limestone, hard, compact, silicious, and of a dirty gray color.

VI. *Snow Shoe Basin*, Freeport limestone. (Shaft of Bellefonte and Snow Shoe railroad.) (R. P., 1874, H, p. 76.)

Limestone, hard and highly silicious, and with conchoidal fracture.

Clearfield County.

	VII.	VIII.
Carbonate of lime	93.810	91.880
Carbonate of magnesia	1.710	1.892
Sulphur	.053	.135
Phosphorus	.008	.031
Insoluble residue	2.070	2.770

VII. *Caldwell's Opening*, one mile west of Glenn Hope. (R. P., 1874, H, p. 105.)

Limestone, hard, compact, and of a bluish gray color.

VIII. *Owen's Opening*, on Clearfield creek, one mile east of Clearfield. (R. P., 1874, H, p. 98.)

Limestone, highly crystalline, of a deep blue color.

Elk County.

	IX.	X.
Carbonate of lime	66.912	36.764
Carbonate of magnesia	9.836	2.011
Sulphur	.118	trace.
Phosphorus	.072	.031
Insoluble residue	16.130	53.330

IX. *Pearsall's (Goff's) Run*, one mile north of Caledonia. (R. P., 1874, H, p. 139.)

Limestone, hard, compact, crystalline, bluish gray color, conchoidal fracture, and showing crystals of pyrites.

X. *Pearsall's (Goff's) Run*. Second sample. (R. P., 1874, H, p. 139.)

Limestone, hard, very sandy, and of a bluish gray color.

York County.

	XI.	XII.	XIII.	XIV.
Carbonate of lime	73.180	62.350	77.890	93.870
Carbonate of magnesia	4.370	6.320	2.830	.960
Iron	.520	5.270	1.330	.300
Insoluble residue	21.500	20.060	15.890	4.300

XI. *In bottom of M' William's Slope*, one mile north-east from Dillsburg.

Limestone conglomerate, crystalline; color greenish gray.

XII. *Opposite Allison's Mill*, Xenia P. O., five miles south-east from Hanover.

Limestone, including fragments of chlorite slate, greenish gray color, with considerable adhering oxide of iron. Contains a considerable amount of manganese.

XIII. *In Shaft No.* 5, three-fourths of a mile north-east from Mt. Alto furnace, Franklin county.

Conglomerate limestone from heading of drift.

XIV. *Half a mile south of Seitzland,* in railroad cut, five miles north of Maryland line, Northern Central railroad.

White crystalline limestone, enclosing fragments of chlorite slate.

CHAPTER IV.
FIRE-CLAYS.
Method of Analysis.

1. *Silica.*—One gramme of the finely pulverized clay is fused with six grammes of carbonate of soda over a Bunsen burner, until fusion is complete. The fused mass is then dissolved out in water, acidulated with hydrochloric acid, and evaporated to dryness with the addition of a few drops of nitric acid; re-dissolved in dilute hydrochloric acid, and the silica filtered off, washed thoroughly with hot water, dried, ignited and weighed.

2. *Iron and Alumina.*—The iron and alumina in the solution are then precipitated by means of a *slight excess* of ammonia, the solution boiled, and the precipitate filtered off. After being thoroughly washed with hot water, it is dried, ignited and weighed. This result gives the oxide of iron and alumina. By dissolving the ignited precipitate in hydrochloric acid, the amount of iron present may be estimated by means of a standard solution of bichromate of potash, first taking the precaution to reduce the iron to the state of protochloride by zinc. Where, however, only a small amount of iron is present, it is found best to effect the separation by means of caustic potash. By repeating the separation, the oxide of iron is obtained perfectly free from alumina. Before burning off the oxide of iron, it is first re-dissolved in acid and precipitated with ammonia. The weight of this precipitate is ascertained and deducted from the total iron and alumina, and the difference put down as alumina.

3. *Lime.*—The filtrate from the precipitation of the iron and alumina by ammonia, is boiled for some time with oxalate of

ammonia. The solution after being allowed to stand aside for some time, is then filtered from the oxalate of lime, which is washed well with hot water, dried and ignited; it is then moistened with a solution of carbonate of ammonia, and heated until the last traces of the volatile salt have been expelled. It is weighed as carbonate, from which the per cent of lime is calculated. Where a considerable amount of lime is present, the method of estimation as given for limestones is preferable, but where only a small quantity exists in the substance under examination, the above method is much shorter and is equally reliable.

4. *Magnesia.*—The magnesia is estimated in the filtrate from the lime by precipitating it in a strongly ammoniacal solution by means of the phosphate of soda.

5. *Water.*—One gramme of the clay, in powder, is heated in a glass tube to a dull red heat, and the water collected in a counterpoised chloride of calcicum tube, the increase in weight of which gives the amount of water present.

6. *Alkalies.*—One gramme of the finely pulverized clay is intimately mixed with an equal weight of chloride of ammonium; eight parts by weight of carbonate of lime are then added, and the whole thoroughly mixed. The mixed mass is then transferred to a large platina crucible, and heated cautiously until all the ammoniacal salts are expelled. The heat is now increased until the crucible becomes red hot, at which temperature it is kept for about an hour. The crucible and contents are then put into a beaker with hot water; the mass soon separates from the crucible, which may now be taken out and washed thoroughly. The mixture is allowed to digest at a moderate heat for some time, when the solution is filtered. The filtrate is treated with an excess of carbonate of ammonia, then concentrated by evaporation, after which some more carbonate of ammonia and a little caustic ammonia are added to precipitate the last traces of the lime. The solution is now filtered into a tared platina capsule, a few drops of sulphuric acid added, and the whole evaporated to dryness. The residue, in the dish, is now cautiously heated over a gas flame until the salts of ammonia have volatilized; it is then moistened with a solution of carbonate of ammonia, after which it is heated to a dull red so as

to drive off all salts of ammonia. The capsule is then transferred to the desiccator, where it is allowed to cool. The weight is then taken and the increase noted as sulphates of the alkalies. Sometimes a small amount of insoluble residue is present, which must be deducted from the total weight of the sulphates. The sulphuric acid is estimated by dissolving the mass in water, with a little hydrochloric acid, and precipitating with chloride of barium. By deducting the weight of the sulphuric acid from the weight of the sulphates of the alkalies, the amount of alkalies present in the clay is found. This method was first suggested by Prof. J. Lawrence Smith, and is found to work admirably.

7. *Titanic Acid.*—When titanic acid is present, the clay is decomposed by fusing with bisulphate of soda, the fused mass dissolved out in cold water, and the silica filtered off. It was found that long protracted boiling was insufficient to precipitate the titanic acid from this solution. By first precipitating with ammonia and afterwards dissolving in sulphuric acid, the precipitation of titanic acid by boiling is almost immediate and complete. By this method the titanic acid is obtained perfectly free from impurity.

8. *Sulphuric Acid and Sulphur.*—These are determined by the same processes as given for iron ores. The sulphur existing as sulphuric acid is deducted from the total sulphur, and the residue calculated as iron pyrites, (bisulphide of iron.)

Centre County.

	I.	II.	III.	IV.
Silica	45.650	44.950	45.820	74.950
Alumina	34.730	37.750	35.950	15.940
Protoxide of iron	3.546	2.700	3.320	1.899
Bisulphide of iron	none.	none.	none.	none.
Lime	.112	.302	.112	.106
Magnesia	.619	.216	.573	.407
Alkalies	5.750	.985	4.130	1.756
Sulphuric acid	.165	.075	trace.	.050
Water	9.650	13.050	10.130	4.885
	100.222	100.028	100.045	99.993

I. *Sandy Ridge*, Tyrone and Clearfield railroad, four miles from Osceola, Clearfield county. Top layer. (R. P., 1874, H, p. 119.)

ANALYSES OF FIRE-CLAYS.

Clay, massive, pearl gray color, unctuous; outside of piece slightly fibrous.

II. *Sandy Ridge*, four miles from Osceola. Second layer from top. (R. P., 1874, H, p. 119.)

Clay, compact, grayish color, with bluish tint on fresh fracture.

III. *Sandy Ridge*, four miles from Osceola. Third layer from top. (R. P., 1874, H, p. 119.)

Clay, compact, pearl gray color, containing small scales of mica. Breaks up in blocks.

IV. *Sandy Ridge*, four miles from Osceola. (R. P., 1874, H, p. 119.)

Clay, compact and sandy, pearl gray color, containing small scales of mica.

Clearfield County.

	V.	VI.	VII.	VIII.
Silica	60.130	64.850	50.150	67.950
Alumina	25.710	23.770	35.600	20.150
Protoxide of iron	2.371	1.218	.827	1.960
Bisulphide of iron	.067	.032	.031	.032
Lime	.117	.190	.112	.084
Magnesia	.663	.122	.160	.216
Alkalies	3.490	.345	.070	2.045
Sulphuric acid	.191	.280	.140	.224
Water	7.280	9.560	13.610	6.580
	100.019	100.367	100.700	99.241

V. *Clearfield Fire-Clay Works*; mine at Clearfield. No. 1, two feet average thickness. (R. P., 1874, H, p. 126.)

The clay is hard, compact, and of a slaty color.

VI. *Clearfield Fire-Clay Works*; mine at Clearfield. No. 2, two feet average thickness. (R. P., 1874, H, p. 126.)

The clay is hard, compact, and of a slaty color.

VII. *Clearfield Fire-Clay Works*; mine at Clearfield. No. 3, four feet average thickness. (R. P., 1874, H, p. 126.)

The clay is hard, compact, and of a dark olive color; fracture conchoidal, and structure slightly laminated.

Analyzed by S. A. Ford.

VIII. *Clearfield Fire-Clay Works*; mine at Clearfield. No. 4, two feet average thickness. (R. P., 1874, H, p. 126.)

The clay is hard, compact, and of a dark gray color.

Analyzed by S. A. Ford.

	IX.	X.	XI.	XII.	XIII.
Silica	57.875	53.560	61.000	51.360	61.975
Alumina	27.005	28.820	25.800	31.250	22.260
Protoxide of iron..	2.549	2.243	2.347	1.936	2.696
Bisulphide of iron,	.033	.135	.064	.748	.101
Titanic acid				.500	.385
Lime	.112	.431	trace.	.061	.157
Magnesia	.465	.605	.530	.260	.380
Alkalies	3.170	1.800	2.800	.035	1.795
Sulphuric acid		.869	.379	.381	.240
Water	8.305	11.406	7.792	12.832	9.278
	99.514	99.869	100.712	99.363	99.267

IX. *Clearfield Fire-Clay Works;* mine at Clearfield. No. 5, two feet average thickness. (R. P., 1874, H, p. 126.)

The clay is hard, compact, unctuous, with gray color and slaty structure.

Analyzed by S. A. Ford.

X. *Clearfield Fire-Clay Works;* mine at Clearfield. No. 6, two feet average thickness. (R. P., 1874, H, p, 126.)

The clay is hard, compact and slaty, and of a slightly bluish color.

Analyzed by S. A. Ford.

XI. *Clearfield Fire-Clay Works;* mine at Clearfield. No. 7, four feet average thickness. (R. P., 1874, H, p. 126.)

The clay is hard, brittle, unctuous, and of a gray color.

Analyzed by S. A. Ford.

XII. *Clearfield Fire-Clay Works;* Mine at Clearfield. No. 8, two feet average thickness.

The clay is compact, of a light pearl gray color, with conchoidal fracture.

Analyzed by S. A. Ford.

XIII. *Clearfield Fire-Clay Works;* raw brick.

Analyzed by S. A. Ford.

	XIV.	XV.	XVI.
Silica	42.700	43.350	44.550
Alumina	37.600	37.550	39.000
Protoxide of iron	2.385	2.145	1.440
Titanic acid	2.500	2.825	1.700
Lime	.112	.084	.028
Magnesia	.270	.234	.072
Alkalies	.730	.235	.530
Water	13.840	14.170	13.660
	100.137	100.593	100.980

ANALYSES OF FIRE-CLAYS. M. 83

XIV. *Porter's Mine*, (Harrisburg Fire-clay Works,) three miles west of Blue Ball Station. Tyrone and Clearfield railroad, five miles west of Philipsburg. Upper layer. (R. P., 1874, H, p 121.)

The clay is hard, compact, of a dark bluish gray color.

Analyzed by S. A. Ford.

XV. *Porter's Mine*, Blue Ball Station. Middle layer. (R. P., 1874, H, p. 121.)

The clay is hard, compact, with pearl gray color and conchoidal fracture.

Analyzed by S. A. Ford.

XVI. *Porter's Mine*, Blue Ball Station. Bottom layer. (R. P., 1874, H, p. 121.)

The clay is hard and compact, with light pearl gray color and conchoidal fracture.

Analyzed by S. A. Ford.

	XVII.	XVIII.	XIX.	XX.
Silica	46.250	45.450	45.230	46.180
Alumina	37.500	36.125	38.030	36.880
Protoxide of iron	1.935	2.275	1.980	2.250
Bisulphide of iron	......	......	......	......
Lime	.168	.168	.163	.173
Magnesia	.126	.342	.237	.317
Alkalies	1.115	1.290	.830	2.760
Sulphuric acid	......	......	.013	.009
Water	13.540	13.730	13.605	11.580
	100.634	99.380	100.088	100.149

XVII. *Hope Fire-Clay Mine*, near Woodland P. O., Tyrone and Clearfield railroad. (R. P., 1874, H, p. 123.)

The clay is hard, compact, pearl gray color, and somewhat slaty structure.

Analyzed by S. A. Ford.

XVIII. *Woodland Fire-Clay Works;* mine at north side of Roaring Run brook. (R. P., 1874, H, p. 123.)

The clay is hard, compact, with pearl gray color and slaty structure.

Analyzed by S. A. Ford.

XIX. *Gearhart Clay;* mine about three-fourths of a mile north-west of Woodland station, on the Tyrone and Clearfield railroad. Hard clay. (R. P., 1874, H, p. 124.)

The clay is hard and compact, with slaty color.

XX. *Gearhart Clay;* mine about three-fourths of a mile north-west of Woodland station, on Tyrone and Clearfield railroad. Soft clay. (R. P., 1874, H, p. 124.)

The clay is compact, of a pearl gray color, and comparatively soft.

Jefferson County.

	XXI.	XXII.	XXIII.
Silica	58.125	60.675	78.075
Alumina	26.500	25.915	14.440
Protoxide of iron	3.234	2.210	1.590
Bisulphide of iron	.008	......	......
Lime	.078	.089	.056
Magnesia	.555	.465	.480
Alkalies	2.180	1.925	1.670
Sulphuric acid	.058	trace.	trace.
Water	9.725	9.090	4.163
	100.463	100.369	100.474

XXI. *Newsome Fire-Clay;* three-quarters of a mile south of Brookville. Top layer. (R. P., 1874, H, p. 225.)

Clay is comparatively soft, and of a pearl gray color. Analyzed by S. A. Ford.

XXII. *Newsome Fire-Clay;* middle layer. (R. P., 1874, H, p. 225.)

Clay is compact, unctuous, and of a pearl gray color. Analyzed by S. A. Ford.

XXIII. *Newsome Fire-Clay;* bottom layer. (R. P., 1874, H, p. 225.)

Clay is very sandy, hard, compact, and of a light gray color. Analyzed by S. A. Ford.

Elk county.

	XXIV.	XXV.
Silica	44.450	44.045
Alumina	38.945	39.445
Protoxide of iron	2.135	.940
Lime	.173	.075
Magnesia	.155	.115
Sulphuric acid	trace.	trace.
Alkalies	.760	.720
Water	13.287	14.138
	99.905	99.478

XXIV. *Jones' Mine,* one a half miles west of Benezette. (R. P., 1874, H, p. 134.)

The clay is hard, compact, of a pearl gray color, with conchoidal fracture.
Analyzed by S. A. Ford.

XXV. *E. Fletcher & Brother's Mine,* two miles west of Benezette. (R. P., 1874, H, p. 135.)
Clay is very hard and compact, and of a light gray color.
Analyzed by S. A. Ford.

Notes.—Clays are essentially hydrated silicates of alumina, and on the presence of the water of combination depends their plasticity or capability of being moulded into any given form. Bischof finds that the analysis of a clay gives a distinct indication as to its power of resisting extreme heats. The value of a refractory clay is found by the proportion of alumina to the silica, and again by that of the alumina to the fluxes, (alkalies, alkaline earths and iron oxide.) The more alumina a clay contains in proportion to the fluxes or fusible matter, the more refractory it is; on the other hand, the fusibility of a clay at high temperatures increases directly with the quantity of silica it contains. Of two clays containing the same proportion of alumina to fluxes, the one containing relatively less silica will be found to resist heat better. Save in the case of a few well defined exceptions—dependent upon certain external properties of the clays—it was found that clays having the same proportions of aluminous and silicious constituents, possessed an equal power of resisting extreme heats.

The principal impurities in clays are oxide of iron, lime, magnesia, alkalies, and sometimes a small amount of iron pyrites. The presence of these in considerable quantity renders the clay incapable of withstanding a high temperature without fusion. Fire-bricks, formed of baked clay, must be able to withstand sudden changes of temperature without fracture, and extreme degrees of heat without fusion.

In order to afford a convenient comparison of the clays from this State with other standard clays, the analyses here given in detailed form are grouped together in a table, followed by tables giving the analyses of standard British clays and others from the Continent of Europe.

PENNSYLVANIA FIRE CLAYS.

	Silica	Alumina	Protoxide of iron	Bisulphide of iron	Titanic acid	Lime	Magnesia	Alkalies	Sulphuric acid	Water	Total
1. Sandy Ridge, Centre county	45.650	34.730	3.546			.112	.619	5.750	.165	9.650	100.222
2. Sandy Ridge do	44.950	37.750	2.700			.302	.216	.985	.075	13.050	100.028
3. Sandy Ridge do	45.820	35.950	3.330			.112	.573	4.130	trace.	10.130	100.045
4. Sandy Ridge do	74.950	15.940	1.899			.106	.407	1.756	.950	4.885	99.993
5. Clearfield Fire-clay Works	60.130	25.710	2.371	.067		.117	.663	3.490	.191	7.280	100.019
6. Clearfield do	64.850	23.770	1.218	.032		.190	.122	.345	.280	9.650	100.367
7. Clearfield do	50.150	35.600	.827	.031		.112	.160	.070	.140	13.610	100.700
8. Clearfield do	67.950	20.150	1.960	.032		.084	.216	2.045	.224	6.580	99.241
9. Clearfield do	57.875	27.065	2.549	.033		.112	.465	3.170		8.350	99.514
10. Clearfield do	53.560	28.820	2.243	.135		.431	.605	1.800	.869	11.406	99.869
11. Clearfield do	61.000	25.800	2.347	.064	.500	trace.	.530	2.800	.379	7.792	100.712
12. Clearfield do	51.360	31.250	1.936	.748	.385	.061	.260	.035	.381	12.832	99.363
13. Clearfield do	61.975	22.260	2.696	.101		.157	.380	1.795	.240	9.278	99.267
14. Blue Ball	42.700	37.600	2.385		2.500	.112	.270	.730		13.840	100.137
15. Blue Ball	43.350	37.550	2.145		2.825	.084	.234	.235		14.170	100.593
16. Blue Ball	44.550	39.000	1.440		1.700	.028	.072	.530		13.650	100.980
17. Woodland Station	46.250	37.500	1.935			.168	.126	1.115	.013	13.540	100.634
18. Woodland Station	45.450	36.125	2.275			.084	.342	1.290	.009	13.730	99.380
19. Woodland Station	45.230	38.030	1.980			.168	.237	.830	.058	13.605	100.088
20. Woodland Station	46.180	35.880	2.250			.163	.317	2.760		11.580	100.149
21. Newsome Fire-clay	58.125	26.500	3.234	.008		.173	.555	2.180		9.725	100.463
22. Newsome do	60.675	25.915	2.210			.078	.465	1.925	trace.	9.090	100.369
23. Newsome do	78.075	14.440	1.590			.089	.480	1.670	trace.	4.163	100.474
24. Jones do	44.450	38.945	2.135			.056	.155	.760	trace.	13.287	99.905
25. E. Fletcher & Bro., Fire-clay	44.045	39.445	.940			.173	.115	.720	trace.	14.138	99.478

ANALYSES OF FIRE-CLAY.   M. 87

COMPOSITION OF BRITISH FIRE-CLAYS.

	1.	2.	3.	4.	5.	6.	7.	8.	9.	10.	11.	12.	13.	14.	15.
Silica	63.30	51.80	50.20	51.10	69.25	55.50	67.12	53.05	58.10	66.16	79.40	68.98	42.00	59.49	45.25
Alumina	23.30	30.40	32.59	31.85	17.90	27.75	21.18	28.13	26.59	22.54	12.25	23.82	40.90	28.95	28.27
Protoxide of iron	1.80	4.14			2.97	2.01				5.31		.10	trace	1.05	
Sesquioxide of iron			3.52	4.63		.67	1.85	2.48	2.97		1.30	.39			7.72
Lime	.73		.36	1.46	1.30	.75	.32	.17	.40	1.42	.50	trace	1.30	trace	.47
Magnesia		.50	.44	1.54		2.19	.84	1.20	.99	trace		.17	.10		
Potash			2.32			.44	2.02	4.19	1.21			.07			
Soda		trace										.49			
Water, combined			9.69	10.47	7.58	10.53	4.82	5.82	7.57	3.14	5.20	5.54	14.70	11.05	17.34
Water, hygroscopic	10.30	13.11					1.39	2.20	1.41			.85			
Organic matter							.90	2.82	1.21						
	99.43	99.95	99.12	100.55	99.00	99.84	100.44	100.06	100.45	98.57	98.65	100.41	99.00	100.54	99.05

1. Stourbridge, Worcestershire; used for glass pots; by C. Tookey. 2. Brierley Hill, Staffordshire; by T. H. Henry. 3. Glascote, near Tamworth; by J. Spiller. 4, 5. Newcastle on Tyne; by T. Richardson. 6. Newcastle on Tyne; by Hugh Taylor. 7, 8, 9. Dowlais, South Wales; by E. Riley; No. 7 is considered the best fire-clay of the district. 10. Glasgow; by J. Brown. 11. Ireland; by T. H. Henry; clay of excellent quality. 12. Lee Moor, Devon; by J. A. Phillips. 13. Clay from Stannington; by Le Play. 14. Clay from the iron works at Gartsherrie; by Schwarz. 15. Clay from Stourbridge; by Salvétat.

COMPOSITION OF FIRE-CLAYS FROM THE CONTINENT OF EUROPE.

	1.	2.	3.	4.	5.	6.	7.	8.	9.	10.	11.	12.	13.	14.	15.
Silica, combined	63.57	60.60	66.10	32.08	36.04	32.70	59.01	60.40	54.06	46.50	55.46	77.32	56.00	52.00	47.50
Silica, as sand				25.04	21.04	26.40							2.00	9.80	34.37
Alumina	27.45	26.39	19.80	29.06	30.04	27.46	24.26	24.09	26.99	34.90	31.74	15.57	26.00	25.00	1.24
Sesquioxide of iron	.15	2.50	6.30	.45	.67	.93	4.04	3.70	2.73	3.00	.59	.86			.50
Lime	.55	.84		.04	.56	.10	1.32	.55	.85		.19	trace.			1.00
Magnesia	trace.			.70	.18	.34	.72	.61	.82		.14	.13	2.00	trace.	
Potash									.24		2.49	.67			
Soda		9.20	7.50	1.14	2.10	2.40	1.20	.29	.33		.68	.63			
Water, combined	8.64			9.03	8.45	8.00	10.24	.22	14.15	13.30	9.37	5.61	14.00	12.60	14.43
Water, hygroscopic	1.27							10.60							
	101.63	99.53	99.70	97.54	99.08	98.33	100.79	100.46	100.17	97.70	100.66	100.79	100.00	99.40	99.04

1. Beleu, Ardennes. 2. Dourdan, Seine-et-Oise. 3. Hayanges, Moselle; by Salvétat; No. 3 used for fire-bricks. 4, 5, 6. Clays from Belgium; by Bischof. 7. Schöningen, Hanover; by Streng. 8, 9. Kipfendorf, Saxe-Coburg; by Fresenius. 10. Almerode, Hessen-Cassel; by Berthier. 11. Vallendar, near Coblenz. 12. Mehlem, near Königswinter. 13. Tahier, Belgium; by Coste. 14. Mazet, Belgium; by Coste. 15. Almerode, Hesse; makes excellent crucibles; by Salvétat.

The above tables were taken from Phillips' "Elements of Metallurgy" and Crookes & Röhrigs' "Steel and Fuel."

CHAPTER V.

MISCELLANEOUS ANALYSES.

	I.
Protoxide of iron	45.064
Sesquioxide of iron	1.553
Bisulphide of iron	.457
Alumina	1.643
Protoxide of manganese	1.150
Lime	.644
Magnesia	1.495
Carbonic acid	29.330
Phosphoric acid	.142
Sulphuric acid	.061
Water	.420
Insoluble residue	17.575
	99.534
Iron	36.350
Sulphur	.268
Phosphorus	.062

I. *Barber's Mine*, Hensingerville; one and a half miles from Alburtis. (R. P., 1874, D, p. 22.)

Carbonate ore, hard and compact; surface white, brownish color on fresh fracture; laminated structure and minutely crystalline. This ore is found underneath the brown hematite, and occurs in white rounded balls of considerable weight and various sizes. It has, however, only been found in small quantities.

	II.
Protoxide of iron	16.303
Sesquioxide of iron	63.366
Bisulphide of iron	.137
Alumina	2.970
Protoxide of manganese	2.414
Lime	1.428
Magnesia	2.397
Carbonic acid	.850
Sulphuric acid	.485
Phosphoric acid	.208
Water	3.170
Insoluble residue	6.460
	100.188

```
Iron .................................................. 57.100
Sulphur ................................................ .267
Phophorus .............................................. .091
Manganese ............................................. 1.730
```

II. *Mechling's Mine*, mined by Lehigh Valley Iron Company. Hard and compact magnetite, considerably oxidized, sample containing a large admixture of fine ore.

III.
```
Ferrous oxide......................   5.142 }
Ferric oxide.......................  65.716 } =50.000 per cent iron.
Manganous oxide....................  trace.
Alumina............................   4.032
Lime...............................   3.836
Magnesia...........................    .256
Phosphoric acid....................    .139=0.060 per ct. phosphorus.
Sulphuric acid.....................  trace.
Insoluble residue..................  20.800
                                     ───────
                                     99.921
```

III. *D. V. Ahl's Ore*, Adams county. Average from lot received at Pennsylvania Steel Works.

Analysis published by permission of S. M. Felton, Esq., President.

IV.
```
Protoxide of iron ................  22.536 }
Sesquioxide of iron ..............  50.080 } =52.58 per cent iron.
Alumina...........................   2.560
Protoxide of manganese............  trace.
Oxide of copper...................    .500
Oxide of cobalt...................  trace.
Lime .............................   1.208
Magnesia..........................   5.172
Phosphoric acid...................  trace.
Sulphur...........................    .180
Water.............................    .780
Silica............................  16.440
                                    ───────
                                    99.456
```

IV. *Cornwall Surface Ore*; average at Robesonia. Analyzed by Mr. Andrew A. Blair in 1871, in the Laboratory of Messrs. Booth & Garrett. This analysis is given to compare with the "Mumper," "Fuller" and "Dillsburg" ores. It will be noticed that the general character of the ores is the same. The average Cornwall ore is generally richer in sulphur and copper than is shown in the above analysis of the *surface ore*.

An analysis of pig iron made from the Cornwall ore is given underneath.

```
                                               V.
Graphitic carbon....................................  3.360
Combined carbon.....................................   .763
Silicium............................................ 1.742
Sulphur.............................................   .071
Phosphorus..........................................   .072
Manganese ..........................................   .576
Copper.............................................. 1.200
Calcium.............................................   .056
Magnesium .......................................... trace.
Aluminium...........................................   .427
Iron................................................ 91.679
                                                     ───────
                                                      99.946
```

V. *Cornwall Pig Iron;* average No. 2, quite gray. Analyzed by me in 1871 for Pennsylvania Steel Company, and published by permission of S. M. Felton, Esq., President, to whom the Survey is indebted for many analyses.

Note.—The method for the complete analysis of irons, steels, &c., containing *small quantities* of Carbon, Aluminium and Chromium, will be reserved for next year's report.

```
                                                VI.
Silica..............................................  97.100
Ferric oxide........................................   1.250
Alumina.............................................   1.390
Lime................................................    .179
Magnesia............................................    .129
                                                      ───────
                                                      100.048
```

VI. *Chickies Rock,* near Chickies Station, Pennsylvania Railroad. Quartzite sandstone used at Pennsylvania Steel Works for lining the Bessemer Converters.

Analysis published by permission of S. M. Felton, Esq., President.

```
                                                VII.
Silica..............................................  63.310
Alumina.............................................  16.160
Ferric oxide........................................   3.790
Lime................................................    .150
Magnesia............................................   4.443
Potash..............................................   7.560
Soda................................................   1.540
Sulphuric acid......................................    .110
Phosphoric acid.....................................    .102
Water...............................................   2.650
                                                      ───────
                                                       99.815
```

VII. *Damourite Slate*, from Hensinger Heirs' Mine at Hensingerville. (R. P., 1874, D. p. 12.)

Yellowish white color, slaty structure, and somewhat soapy feel, very soft and easily broken.

	VIII.	IX.
Silica	55.880	60.530
Alumina	19.400	17.400
Oxide of Iron	10.570	9.290
Lime	.080	.080
Magnesia	1.710	1.920
Water	8.170	5.510
Alkalies	3.760	5.270
	99.570	100.000

VIII. *Ochre* from Nathan Whiteley's Mud-dam, one mile from Trexlertown, on road to Breinigsville, Lehigh county. (R. P., 1874, D, p. 35.)

Ochre, soft but compact, sandy, and of a light brown color.

IX. *Ochre* from Francis Breinig's Mine, one and one-half miles north, north-west of Breinigsville, Lehigh county. Dried ochre. (R. P., 1874, D, p. 33.)

Ochre, soft but compact, sandy, and of a very light brown color.

	X.	XI.	XII.
Silica	76.100	57.590	48.835
Alumina	10.040	19.297	25.235
Protoxide of iron	3.493	6.429	2.279
Bisulphide of iron	.043	......	.198
Lime	.683	1.285	.165
Magnesia	1.419	1.502	.635
Alkalies	2.460	1.970	1.780
Sulphuric acid	.151	.016	.334
Water	5.390	12.049	3.090
Organic matter	.110	......	17.794
	99.889	100.138	100.345

X. *Lewistown Section*, clay attached to carbonate ore taken from near the surface, one mile north-west of Lewistown, Mifflin county.

The clay is soft and of a pearl gray color.

XI. *Clay from Gnist's Meadow*, one-quarter mile south-west of Wellsville, York county.

The clay is very soft and of a light blue color.

Analyzed by S. A. Ford.

XII. *Roof Slate of Coal* from bed of Sandy Creek, Reynoldsville, Jefferson county. (R. P., 1874, H, p. 198.)

The slate is hard and compact, of a deep black color, and showing numerous crystals of pyrites.

Analyzed by S. A. Ford.

	XIII.
Silica	45.880
Alumina	33.920
Protoxide of iron	4.680
Lime	.160
Magnesia	.750
Alkalies	4.643
Water	10.370
	100.403

XIII. *Sandy Ridge fire-clay*, average sample as used by the Pennsylvania Steel Company. (R. P., 1874, H, p. 119.)

Analysis made in 1870 and published by permission. By comparing the above analysis with those made for Mr. Franklin Platt's report during the past season, the extreme regularity of this clay is apparent

XIV.

	Carbon.	Sulphur.	Ash.
1871	86.010	1.110	12.880
1873	88.869	1.126	10.005
1873	89.378	0.872	9.750
1871*	89.600	1.080	9.320
1871*	87.940	1.180	10.880
1874*		0.768	

Analyses of Connelsville Coke, made by George Hay, for Lucy Furnace Co., Pittsburgh; and published by their kind permission.

NOTE.—The labels given with the analyses in this report were furnished for the most part by the different assistant geologists; those from the bituminous coal district, including coals, ores, limestones and clays, by Mr. Franklin Platt, Report H; those from Lehigh county, by Professor Frederick Prime, Jr., Report D; those from York and Adams counties, by Prof. Persifor Frazer, Jr., Report C; and those from Mifflin and Huntingdon counties, by Mr. John H. Dewees, Report F.

---
* Washed coke.

INDEX

To Report of Progress in the Laboratory, at Harrisburg, by Andrew S. M'Creath, Chemical Assistant.

	PAGE.
Ahl's (D. V.) ore, Adams county	90
Alburtis, ores near	49, 50, 51, 54, 76, 89
Alkalies in clay, estimation of	79
Allegheny Mountain ore	69
Allentown Iron Company	50, 51
Allentown Rolling Mill Company	49
Allison's mill, limestone opposite	77
Almerode, Hessen-Cassel, clay, analysis	88
Alumina, estimation of, in ores, 46; clays	78
Aluminium in pig iron	91
Analyses, tables of, of coals, 3–23; coal ashes, 27; cokes, 24; phosphoric acid in coals, 25; iron and sulphur in coals, 26; iron ores, 48–74; limestones, 75–78; clays, 80–88; miscellaneous	89–93
Analysis of coals, method of, 2; of ores, 43; of limestones, 75; clays	78
Anthony's coal mine	17, 39
Anthracite, weather waste in, 34; used as fuel	48
Armstrong county coals, analyses of	18–20
Ash in coal, average percentage of, 29; phosphoric acid in, 29; value as a fertilizer, 30; method of estimation	2
Barber (J.) & Co.'s mine, 49; carbonate ore	89
Barnhart's ore bank	65
Bastian's (Elwyn) ore mine	51
Beaver Branch of Moshannon river	4
Beleu, Ardennes, clay, analysis	88
Belgium clays, analyses	88
Bell's coal mine	10, 39
Bellefonte and Snow Shoe railroad	69, 76
Bell township, coal mine in	9
Benezette coals, analyses of, 21, 22; clays	84, 85
Bennett's Branch Low Grade railroad	10
Bessemer pig iron, ores suitable for, 55; purity of fuel required for	29
Bishop's Summit, coal near	21
Bituminous coals, definition and classification of, 1; weather waste in, 33–37; tables of analyses	38–40
Blackband ores, analyses of	74
Black carbonate ore, analysis of	70
Blacklog Gap ores	63
Blacklog mountain, ores on	63, 66, 67
Blair's (Andrew A.) analysis	90
Blair county coals, analyses of	22
Blank's ore mine	50

[M. 95.]

INDEX.

	PAGE.
Blue Ball station fire-clays	83, 86
Bog, analysis of	67
Bog ore, analysis of	66
Bollinger ore bank, 55; insoluble residue	59
Bombshell ore	50
Booth & Garrett's analysis, 4; laboratory	90
Bortz's (Alwyn) ore mine	52
Bovaird's ore	69
Breinig's (Francis) ore mine, 51; ochre	92
Breinig's (Thomas) ore mine	51
Breinigsville, ores near, 51, 52; ochre	92
Brierley Hill clay, analysis of	87
Broad Top	30
Brockwayville	18, 69, 73
Brookville coal, 20; fire clay	84
Brown's coal mine, 14, 40; iron and sulphur in	26
Brown hematite ores, analyses of, Lehigh county, 48–54; Juniata, 64–67; Coal Measures	68, 69
Brunswick, Varrentrapp of	33
Caldwell's limestone	77
Caledonia coal, 22; limestone	77
Calhoun's (W. J.) coal mine	18, 40
Caloric, per cent lost by weather waste of coal	36
Cambrian (?) and Mesozoic, ores of the	55
Cannel coal, analyses of	19
Cannelton (Ia.) coal, analysis of	42
Canoe township coal, 22; ore	74
Carbon Iron Company's ores	51, 52
Carbonate of lime in coal, 32; in fossil ores	60
Carbonate ores, Juniata, 69–71; Coal Measures	71–74
Carbonate ore found with brown hematite, 89; analysis of hematite	49
Carbonate of soda, sulphur in	3
Carbonic acid, estimation of	47
Centre county coals, 10, 11, 39; clays, 80; limestones, 76; brown hematite ores, 69; carbonate ores	72
Chauvenet's (Regis) analyses	28
Chert ore bank	66
Chestnut Ridge ores	66, 67, 71
Chesterfield Mining Company's coal	42
Chickies rock, 91; station	91
Chlorite slate in limestone	77
Chloritic rock	57
Clarion county coals, analyses of, 20, 40; carbonate ore	74
Clay attached to carbonate ore, analysis of	92
Clayband ore	72
Clayville iron ore	73
Clearfield	8, 9, 26, 77, 81, 82
Clearfield creek	9, 68, 73, 77
Clearfield county coals, 3–10, 38, 39; brown hematite ores, 68; carbonate ores, 73; limestones, 77; clays	81–86
Clearfield Fire-clay Works, clays of	81, 82

	PAGE.
Clinton shales, iron ore in	67
Clover Hill coal, analysis of	42
Coals, classification of, 1; bituminous, 1; semi-bituminous, 1; coking, 1; free-burning, 1; tables of analyses, 38–42; method of analysis, 2; average per cent water, 28 volatile matter, 30; fixed carbon, 30; ash, 29; sulphur, 30; condition of the sulphur, 31; iron and sulphur in, 26; phosphoric acid in, 25,29; carbonate of lime, 32; ash, analyses of	27
Coal Measures, brown hematite ores of, 68,69; red hematite ore in, 68; carbonate ores, 71–74; limestone	76, 77
Coal, roof slate of	93
Cobalt in iron ores	58
Coblenz clay, analysis of	88
Codorus ore, analysis of	58
Cokes, tables of analyses	24, 93
Coke, natural, analysis of	42
Coking coals	1
Coleraine Iron Company's ores	49, 53
Conglomerate limestone	77, 78
Connellsville coke	93
Cooper's (J.) coal mine	9, 38
Cornwall surface ore, 90; pig iron	91
Crane Iron Company's ores	52, 54
Creek Company's coal	42
Creek, Sandy, coal from bed of	17
Creek, Toby, coal	18
Crookes & Röhrig, tables of analyses	88
Crouch & Snead's coal	42
Damourite slate, analysis of	92
Dauphin and Susquehanna coal	42
Davis' (G. W.) coal mine	8, 38
Decatur Coal Company's colliery, 6,38; phosphoric acid in coal, 25; iron and sulphur in, 26; ash, analysis of, 27; coke	24
Derby colliery	6, 38, 25
Devonian, brown hematites of the	48
Dewees, (J. H.)	93
Diamond colliery, 11,12,39; phosphoric acid in, 25; ash in, 29; coke	24
Dillsburg ores, 58,59,90; limestone near	77
Douglas ore bank	67
Dourdon, Seine-et-Oise, clay	88
Dowlais clays	87
Dull & Bradley's ore mine	64, 65
Dunkard church, ore near	65
Early & Killinger's ore bank	56, 59
Elk county coals, 21; limestones, 77; clays	84
Emmitsburg road, ore near	57
Engineering and Mining Journal	33
Eureka coal mine, 4,38; phosphoric acid in, 25; iron and sulphur in, 26; ash, analysis of	27
Evergreen station, coal near	10

98 M. INDEX.

	PAGE.
Fairmount colliery	20, 30, 40
Felton, (S. M.)	54, 59, 90, 91
Fergusson Valley ores	60, 61, 62, 65
Ferriferous limestones	60
Fire-bricks, essential qualities of	85
Fire-clays, method of analysis, 78; Pennsylvania, tables of analyses, 86; British, 87; clays from the Continent of Europe, 88; refractory qualities of, what constitutes, 85; titanic acid in	80, 82
Fisher's (Francis) ore mine	53
Fixed carbon in coal, average per cent of	30
Fletcher (E.) & Bro's fire-clay	85
Fogelsville, ores near	53, 54
Fogel's (Wm. B.) ore mine	52
Ford's (S. A.) analyses	62, 63, 65, 67, 81, 82, 83, 84, 85, 92, 93
Forman's (F. W.) analyses	72, 74
Forest county coal, analysis of	23
Fossil ores of the Juniata, analyses of	60-63
Franklin colliery, 3, 38; iron and sulphur in, 26; weather waste of coal,	35
Franklin county limestone	78
Frantz's limestone quarry	76
Frazer, Jr., (Prof. Persifor)	48, 93
Free-burning coals	1
Freeport limestones	76
Fritz's ore bank	56, 59
Fuller's ore bank	58, 90
Gackenbach's ore mine	52
Galusha's (P.) coal mine, 18, 40; iron and sulphur in, 26; sulphur, condition of, 31, 32; carbonate ore	73
Gartsherrie clay	87
Gas coal, weather waste of	34, 36
Gearhart fire-clay	83, 84
German Railway Association's experiments on weather waste of coal	34, 36
Gettysburg, ore near	57
Geological survey, Missouri, 28; Ohio	30
Glascote clay	87
Glasgow, 72; clay	87
Glen Hope coal, 9; brown hematite ore, 68; carbonate ore, 73; limestone	77
Gnist's meadow, clay from	92
Goff's run limestone	77
Goss run coal	5
Graff's (G.) coal mine	22
Grundman's experiments on weather waste of coal	33
Guth's (Francis) ore mine	51
Haldeman's ore bank	55, 59
Hale's colliery	5, 38
Hanover	55, 58, 59, 77
Hanover Junction railroad	58
Harrisburg Fire-clay Works, clays	83
Hawk's coal mine	15, 39
Hay's (George) analyses	93

	PAGE.
Hayanges, Mosselle, clay	88
Help ore bank	57
Hensinger Heir's farm ore bank	50
Hensinger Heir's mine, damourite slate in	92
Hensinger & Saul's mine	50
Hensingerville	49, 50, 89, 92
Hick's ore bank	67
Hime's carbonate ore	74
Hill's coal mine	8, 38
Hill Valley ores	66, 67, 68, 71
Hocking Valley, Ohio, red hematite in	68
Hog Shanty Run ore	73
Holt's Hill	11
Holt's (William) coal mine, 11, 39; phosphoric acid in	25
Hoover's coal mine, 12, 39; phosphoric acid in, 25; iron and sulphur in, 26; ash, analysis of, 27; coke	24
Hope fire-clay mine	83
Houtzdale coals	3, 4, 24, 25, 26, 27
Hubler's coal mine	7, 39
Hum's coal mine	16, 26, 29, 39, 40
Humphrey's coal mine	9, 38
Hunt, (Dr. T. Sterry)	68
Huntingdon county, fossil ores of, 63; brown hematite ores of, 66; carbonate ores	71
Hydro-carbons in coal, loss by exposure to the weather	33
Indiana, coals of	34
Indiana county coals, 22; carbonate ore	74
Insoluble residue in iron ores, estimation of, 44; tables of analyses	59
Iowa coals, per cent of water in	28
Ireland clay	87
Iron, estimation of, in ores	46
Iron ores, method of analysis, 43; tables of analyses, Lehigh county brown hematites, Silurian, 48-54; York county, Cambrian (?) and Mesozoic, 55-59; Juniata fossil ores, Silurian, 60-63; Juniata brown hematites, Devonian 64-68; brown hematites of the Coal Measures, 68, 69; carbonate ores of the Juniata, Devonian, 69-71; carbonate ores of the Coal Measures	71-74
Iron and sulphur in coals, tables of analyses	26
Iron pyrites in coal	36, 37
Jack's Mountain ores	64, 67
Jack's Narrows ore	67
Janesville coal	8
Jefferson county coals, 11-18; brown hematite ores, 68; carbonate ores, 73; clays	84
Johnson's (Prof. W.) tables of analyses, &c	37, 41, 42
Jones' fire-clay	84
Juniata fossil ores, 60-63; brown hematites, 64-67; carbonate ores	69-71
Kaiser's (Harry) ore mine	48
Kansas ores	64, 66
Karthaus coal	42
Karthaus Post-office, coal near, 8; ore	73

INDEX.

	PAGE.
Key's coal mine	18, 40
Kinzer's (John) ore bank	61
Kipfendorf, Saxe-Coburg, clay	88
Knight, (David)	4
Koch's (William) ore mine	52
Kreischmann's (Jonas) ore mine	49
Kroemlich & Lichtenwalner's ore	54
Kuhn's (Mrs.) limestone quarry	76
Kylertown, coal near	7, 8
Lambert's ore	68
Lane's ore bank	66, 67
Lanigan's (James) ore mine	53
Laro's (Jesse) ore mine	54
Lauer's (Milton) ore mine	51
Laurel Run colliery, 6, 38; phosphoric acid in, 25; coke	24
Lee Moor, Devon, Clay	87
Lehigh county brown hematite ores, 48–54; limestones, 76; carbonate ore	89
Lehigh Iron Company's ores	49, 51
Lehigh Valley furnaces, ores used in	48
Lehigh Valley Iron Company's ores	53, 90
Leightner's ores	68, 73
Lewistown, ores near, 64, 65, 70; clay	92
Lewistown section, carbonate ore	70
Lichtenwalner's (Frank S.) ore mine	48, 51
Lichtenwalner's (Levi) ore mine	54
Lime Ridge ore	65
Limestones, method of analysis, 75; Lehigh county, 76; Elk county, 77; York county, 77; Centre county, 76; Clearfield county	77
Limonite, analyses of	48, 55, 64, 68
Littlestown, ore near	56, 59
Liverpool coal	42
Lock ridge, ore near	49
Logan colliery, 5, 38; phosphoric acid in, 25, 29; iron and sulphur in, 26; ash	27
Logan farm ore bank	67, 71
Logan Iron Co.'s ore	65
Logan shaft, Mumper ore	58
London coal mine	17, 40
Low Grade railroad	10, 14, 20, 74
Low Moor, Yorkshire, blackband ore	72, 74
Lucy Furnace Company	93
Ludwig Hertzog & Co.'s ore	50
Ludwig's new mine, 54; old mine	50
Lyken's Valley coal	42
Lyman coal mine, Bishop's Summit	21
Macfarlane, coal regions of America	31
Magnesia, estimation of	45
Magnetic sand	58
Magnetic ores for Bessemer pig iron	55
Mahoning creek, ore in bed of	73

	PAGE.
Manganese, estimation of	44
Mapleton colliery, 4, 38; phosphoric acid in, 25; iron and sulphur in, 26; ash, analysis of, 27; coke	24
Maple Grove mill property ore	49
Marcellus vein ores	65, 71
Marck's (P.) ore mine	49
Margaretta ore bank, 56, 59; furnace	56
Marion, coal near	23
Martin ore bank	67
Maryland line, limestone near	78
Mason's coal mine, 8, 38; iron and sulphur in	26
Matilda furnace ores	62, 63
Mazet, Belgium, clay	88
M'Cord's (John) ore banks	61, 62
M'Creath's (A. S.) analysis of Scotch blackband	74
M'Cullough's (Wm.) coal mine	17, 40
M'Farland's coal mine	22
M'Kean county coals	20
M'Kee's coal mine	16, 39
M'Kee's (Geo.) ore bank	60, 61
M'Master's ore	72
M'Nair's ore	57
M'Veytown, ores near	61, 62, 66
M'Veytown Gap ores	64, 70
M'William's slope, limestone in	77
Mechling's magnetic ore	90
Medina sandstone, ore in	67
Mehlem, Königswinter, clay	88
Midlothian coal	42
Mifflin county fossil ores, 30; brown hematites, 64; carbonate ores	70
Miller's (Chas.) ore mine	53
Millerstown Iron Company's ore	53
Miscellaneous analyses	89–93
Missouri coals, average per cent water in	28
Mon's coal mine	8, 38
Mongold's coal mine, 9, 39; iron and sulphur in	26
Mont Alto furnace, limestone near	78
Moore's ore bank	65
Morrisdale mine, 7, 38; phosphoric acid in, 25; iron and sulphur in, 26; ash, analysis of, 27; coke	24
Moser's (Oliver) ore mine	51
Moshannon colliery, 4, 38; phosphoric acid in	25
Mountain boulder ore	66
Mountain ore bank	67
Mount Union ores	62, 63, 67
Muddy outcrop coal	23
Mull and Hagenbuch's ore	48
Mumper ore bank	58, 90
Navy U. S., Department, tables of experiments	41, 42
Nes Silicon steel ore	57
New Bethlehem	19, 20, 74

	PAGE.
New Castle on Tyne clay	87
New Castle coal	42
New Jersey magnetites	48
New Moshannon coal mine, 4,38; phosphoric acid in	25
New Texas, ore near	50
Newsome's fire-clays	84, 86
Northampton Iron Company's ore	51
Northern Central railroad	57, 78
Norwich Corner coal	21
Notes on iron ore analysis	47, 48
Ochre, analyses of	92
Ohio Company's coal, 12, 25, 26, 27; coke	24
Ohio, coals of, 28, 34; geological survey	30
Orbison slope ores	66, 71
Orbisonia ores,	63, 66, 67, 68, 71
Oriskany sandstone, ores in	65, 66
Oriskany shales, ore in	66
Oriskany Hill ore	64
Osceola	3, 4, 5, 7, 24, 26, 27, 80, 81
Outcrop muddy coal	23
Owen's limestone	77
Oxidation of coal	33
Oxygen, absorption of, by coals	28
Pantal's coal mine	15, 39
Patten's (S.) coal mine	17, 40
Pearsall's (Goff's) run limestones	77
Penn colliery, 3, 38; phosphoric acid in, 25; iron and sulphur in, 26; ash, analysis of, 27; coke	24
Pennsylvania coals, iron and sulphur in	31
Pennsylvania fire-clays, analyses of	86
Pennsylvania railroad	91
Pennsylvania steel company	54, 59, 90, 91, 93
Penny's (Dr.) process for the estimation of iron in ores, 46; laboratory,	72
Petriken colliery	21, 22
Pictou (Cunard's) coal	42
Pictou (New York) coal	42
Pigeon Hill ore	55
Pig iron, analysis of	91
Pipe ore	50, 51
Pittsburg, 93; coal	42
Philipsburg	6, 7, 24, 26, 27, 83
Phillips' Elements of Metallurgy, analyses from	88
Phosphoric acid in coals, 25, 29; estimation of, in ores	43
Plasticity of clay, cause of	85
Platt, (Franklin)	93
Porter's fire-clay mines	83
Powelton coal mine, 7, 38; phosphoric acid in, 25; iron and sulphur in, 26; ash, analysis of	27
Prime, Jr., (Prof. F.)	50, 93
Proximate analysis of coals	2
Quartzite, analysis of	91

	PAGE.
Red Bank coal company's mines	19, 40
Red Bank creek	20, 74
Red hematite in the Coal Measures, 68; Haldeman red oxide, 55; in Blank's mine	50
Reitur's coal mine	8
Remarks on coals, 28; clays	85
Reynold's (D.) coal mine, (Diamond colliery,) 11, 39; phosphoric acid in, 25; coke	24
Reynold's (Woodward) coal mine	13, 40
Reynoldsville	11, 12, 13, 14, 17, 18, 24, 26, 27, 73, 93
Rhodes' (James) ores	64, 66
Richter's (Dr.) experiments on weather waste of coal	33
Roaring Run Brook fire-clay	83
Robesonia	90
Rockdale, coal near	17
Rockhill Coal and Iron Company's ores	63, 66, 67, 71
Romig's (Reuben) ore mine	50
Roof slate of coal	93
Ross ore bank, 64; carbonate ores	69, 70
Rothrick's (John) ore bank	62
Rothwell, (R. P.)	33
Ruth's coal mine	16, 39
Sandy Creek, coal from bed of, 17; roof slate	93
Sandy Ridge ores, 66, 67, 71; fire-clays	80, 81, 86, 93
Schlimmer's iron ore	74
Scholl's (J. D.) & Co.'s ore mine	53
Schöningen, Hanover, clay	88
Scotch blackband ironstone	72, 74
Scotch coal	42
Seitzland, limestone near	78
Seley's coal bank, 14, 39; iron and sulphur in, 26; ash, analysis of	27
Shankweiler's ore mine	49
Sharp's coal mine	14, 15, 40
Shaw's (R.) coal mine	9, 39
Shaw's (J.) coal mine	9, 39
Shehan's (Jas.) ore	60
Shiesley's coal mine	13, 39
Shimmel's run	4, 5, 6, 24, 26
Shrewsbury, ore near	57
Sidney coal	42
Silica, estimation of	47
Silurian ores	48, 60
Slate, damourite, 92; hydro-mica	58
Smith, (Prof. J. L.)	80
Smith's (J. & D.) ore mine	53
Smyser's ore bank	57, 59
Snow Shoe Basin	10, 11, 25, 72, 73, 76
Snow Shoe City	11, 72
Snow Shoe mines	10, 25, 39
Snow Shoe railroad company's colliery, coke from	24
South Wales clays (Dowlais)	87

INDEX.

	PAGE.
Specular iron ore in fossil ore	62
Spiller's (J.) analysis	72, 74
Sprague's coal mine	13, 39
Squaw Hollow, Moore's ore bank	65
Staffordshire clay	87
Stannington clay	87
Steam raising power of coals	41, 42
Stein's (Henry) ore mine	53
Steininger's (Jacob) ore mine	48, 53
Stewart's (J. J.) coal mine	18, 40
Stewart's ore bank	67
Stirling coal mine, 4, 38; phosphoric acid in	25
Stourbridge clays	87
Strickhouser station, ore near	58
Strouse's coal mine	14, 40
Sulphur and iron in coals, tables of analyses	26
Sulphur in coal, estimation of, 2; condition of, 30; average percentage of, 30; sulphur expelled by coking	31
Sulphuric acid, estimation of	43
Surface ore, Cornwall	90
Swartz (Henry) and W. B. Fogel's ore mine	52
Synclinal, first on Lewistown section, carbonate ore	65
Tahier, Belgium, clay	88
Temple Iron Company's ore	49
Thomas' (J.) coal mine	15, 39
Thomas Iron Company's ores, 50, 53; limestone quarry	76
Thompson's (Widow) coal mine	20, 40
Tippecanoe coal	42
Tipton coal, Blair county	23
Titanic acid, estimation of	47, 80
Toby Creek coal, 18; ore	73
Trexlertown	52, 53, 76, 92
Troutville coal	9, 26
Tyler's coal mine, 10, 39; station	10
Tyrone and Clearfield railroad	5, 80, 83, 84
Underwood's (Alex.) ore	59
Vallender, Coblenz, clay	88
Varrentrapp's experiments on weather waste of coals	33
Volatile matter in coal, method of estimation, 2; average percentage	30
Wachob's coal mine	15, 39
Water, estimation of, 2, 43, 79; average percentage in coals, 28; notes on the estimation of	28
Weather waste of coals, 33-37; tables of analyses	35, 36
Weaver's coal mine	15, 26, 39
Webster colliery, 5, 39; phosphoric acid in, 25; iron and sulpher in, 26; small amount of sulphur in	30
Wellsville clay	92
Werner & Reinhart's ore mines	50, 51
Wescoeville ores	51, 53
West Virginia, coals of	34
White, (Prof.)	28

INDEX. M. 105

	PAGE.
Whitely's (Nathan) ore, 52; ochre	92
Whitzel's ore opening	67
Wiand's ore mine	49
Williams' farm, ore on	65
Williamson's coal mine, 7, 38; Run	7
Wilson's farm, ore on	68
Wingert's coal mine	16, 39
Woodland Station	83, 84
Woodland Post Office, clay near	83
Woodland Fire-clay Works, clay	83
Worcestershire clay	87
Wormley, (Prof.)	28, 30, 31
Wrightsville	56, 59
Xenia Post Office, limestone near	77
Yeager's ore	72
Yeagertown ores	60, 61
Yellow Breeches Creek ore	58
York	56, 57, 59
York county iron ores, 55-59; limestones, 77; clay	92
York Iron Company's ore mine	58

Printed in Dunstable, United Kingdom